McCall's
Cookie Collection

BY THE FOOD EDITORS OF McCALL'S

Designed by Margot L. Wolf

PUBLISHED BY ADVANCE PUBLISHERS   P.O. BOX 7200, ORLANDO, FL 32854

Contents

Acknowledgments: The Betsy McCall photographs on page 31 are by Horn/Griner. The photographs on pages 12-13 and 36-37 are by George Lazarnick. All others are by George Ratkai.

Cookies are popular the world round. As a matter of fact, they have a very national character. We in this country have made use of many of the recipes brought to us by settlers, early and late. Our repertoire of cookies is, therefore, rich and varied. Take New England and Virginia cookies. Both areas were settled by men and women from England, and they brought with them the traditional recipes of their country. Gingerbread and ginger cookies have their origin in Germany and England. Some cookies are as personal as a signature. And wild horses couldn't make a woman part with a cherished cookie recipe that has been handed down from mother to daughter in her family.

There are drop cookies and rolled cookies, refrigerator cookies and molded cookies, bar cookies – all quite easy to make, and all keep well in a jar or a covered tin, so you can make them ahead. They keep well, it is true; but we have yet to see the household where *good* cookies remain in the tin more than a few days. What to do then? Simply bake another batch.

Making Cookies

1. Our cookie recipes were tested using *sifted all-purpose flour* – that means sifting the flour before measuring. We specify using *unsifted flour* when the flour may be measured directly from the bag without sifting.

2. When buying baking pans, look for the manufacturer's stamp or mark on each pan, which indicates the size of the pan. Most baking pans today are standardized.

3. If you already have pans that are not marked, measure them from one top inside edge to the opposite inside edge; then mark them yourself.

4. The back of any large baking pan may be substituted for a cookie sheet. Use greased or ungreased, as recipe directs.

5. If you are baking one sheet of cookies at a time, place oven rack in center of oven. If you are baking two sheets, place racks to divide oven into thirds. If tops of cookies do not brown properly, move to a higher rack the last few minutes of baking.

6. Always cool cookie sheet before placing unbaked cookies on it.

7. Check cookies when minimum baking time is up. To cool baked cookies, remove with a wide spatula to wire racks. Do not overlap cookies on racks.

8. Buy two cookie sheets; one sheet of cookies can be baking while the other one is filled. Bright, shiny cookie sheets insure delicately browned cookies. They should be at least an inch shorter and narrower than the oven, to allow for circulation of heat.

Tips for Holiday Baking

Mark special cookie-baking days on your calendar.

Remember that cookies made with honey or fruit, such as Lebkuchen Rounds, may be baked about a month ahead and stored in a cool, dry place (air-tight containers) to mellow.

Rolled ginger cookies and other rolled cookies may be baked about two weeks ahead.

Rich butter cookies and meringue-type cookies are best when baked several days before using.

Chop nuts, slice candied cherries, etc., when you have time, or have available an extra pair of hands in the kitchen. Store in air-tight jars, in a cool place, until needed.

Sift flour and confectioners' sugar onto a square of waxed paper; then measure.

Start a box to hold colored sugar, miniature nonpareils, unusual spices used in holiday cookies, etc., so that when you start making cookies, you'll be sure to have these in the house.

When decorating cookies, keep all your bits of candied fruit, colored sugars, nuts, etc., in individual paper cups or in muffin-pan cups.

To blanch almonds: Cover shelled nuts with cold water; bring to boil. Remove from heat; drain. Press each nut between fingers, so husk will slip off easily. Then drain dry on paper towels.

STORING COOKIES

1. Empty coffee or shortening cans are fine for storing cookies.

2. Line bottom of container with waxed paper; place a sheet of waxed paper between each two layers of cookies. Store crisp and soft cookies in separate containers.

Soft Cookies: Store in container with tight-fitting lid. A slice of apple or bread in the container helps to keep cookies moist. Replace fruit or bread often to prevent mold.

Crisp Cookies: Store in container with loose-fitting lid. If cookies lose their crispness, heat at 300F about 5 minutes before serving.

Bar Cookies: Store right in baking pan. Cover tightly with foil or plastic wrap.

FREEZING COOKIES

Cookies may be frozen either before or after baking. The raw cookie dough is easier to package and takes up less freezer space. However, baking before freezing takes less time and the cookies are ready to eat almost as soon as they come from the freezer.

Both ways are satisfactory. The method followed is entirely up to the individual. Cookies that require a great deal of preparation before baking, like rolled cookies that will be decorated, can be cut and baked ahead. The decorating can be done later, when the cookies are to be used. Meringue-type cookies and frosted cookies are not recommended for freezing.

Store cookies, baked or unbaked, about one month at 0°F or below.

For legible labeling, use a crayon, special pencil, or grease pencil. Be sure to include on the label: name of cookie, date when frozen, oven temperature, and baking time.

Empty coffee and shortening cans are ideal for packing dough or baked cookies. Seal edge with freezer tape, and label.

Freezing Cookie Dough

Drop-cookie dough: Pack dough in 1-pint freezer containers; seal; label; freeze.

To use: Remove from freezer; let stand at room temperature just until dough can be spooned and dropped onto prepared cookie sheet – 30 to 40 minutes. Bake as directed in recipe.

Or drop dough as directed, 1 inch apart, on cookie sheet; freeze, remove solid cookies to freezer containers. Store between layers of waxed paper cut to fit size of container.

To use: Remove from freezer as many as needed. Bake, without thawing, as directed in recipe.

Rolled-cookie dough: Pack dough in 1-pint freezer containers; seal; label; freeze.

To use: Remove from freezer; let stand at room temperature about 10 minutes. Then roll and bake as directed in recipe.

Refrigerator-cookie dough: Form dough into roll, as directed in recipe. Wrap in foil or plastic wrap; seal; label; freeze.

To use: Remove from freezer; remove wrappings. Slice and bake as directed in recipe. Return unused dough (wrapped) to freezer. If dough is brittle, let stand about 5 minutes before slicing.

Or pack dough in empty 6-oz. juice cans, opened at both ends. Seal with foil and freezer tape; label; freeze.

To use: Remove from freezer; remove wrappings; push out dough. Slice and bake as directed in recipe.

Molded-cookie dough: Follow directions for drop-cookie dough, above.

Bar-cookie dough: Fit into 8- or 9-inch square pan a 12-inch square of foil; foil extends over corners. Spread dough in foil-lined pan; freeze, uncovered. Lift out of pan; wrap in foil or plastic wrap; seal; label; freeze.

To use: Remove from freezer; remove wrappings. Bake in pan (used in freezing), without thawing, as directed in recipe.

Freezing Baked Cookies

As soon as cookies are completely cool, pack in freezer containers; seal; label; freeze.

To use: Remove container from freezer. Take out as many cookies as needed (return remaining cookies to freezer, sealed). Let stand at room temperature about 5 minutes.

MAILING COOKIES

Select only cookies that will hold up in the mail. Bar and drop cookies are particularly good for mailing.

Wrap each cookie separately in waxed paper or plastic wrap. Or put in pairs, and wrap each pair.

Line heavy-cardboard box with foil or waxed paper. Pack cookies in box. Stuff corners and any spaces with crushed waxed paper, cotton or marshmallows so cookies are secure; place crushed waxed paper on top of cookies. Cover; secure with tape. Wrap in heavy brown paper; tie securely. Clearly print address and return address. Attach "Fragile" sticker.

Refrigerator Cookies

*T*hese are also called sliced or icebox cookies. They are made from a stiff dough that must be chilled in the refrigerator until it is firm, so it can be sliced as thin and even as possible. The great advantage of refrigerator cookies is that the dough can be kept on hand and the cookies sliced and baked as you need them. They are always crisp, buttery, and flavorful – depending, of course, on the ingredients you use. Our recipes include cinnamon cookies, vanilla cookies, date cookies, and many others. One has that friendly family friend, peanut butter, as an ingredient. Another uses exotic rose water for an unusual flavor.

Shaped Refrigerator Cookies
1. Pack cookie dough in ½-pint cream cartons (with ends removed).
2. Refrigerate until firm – several hours, or overnight.
3. Carefully peel carton away from each roll. With sharp knife, slice dough into ⅛-inch slices, to make squares. Cut each square diagonally, to make triangles. Bake as directed.

HOLLAND ALMOND WAFERS

2¾ cups sifted all-purpose flour
2 teaspoons ground cinnamon
½ teaspoon ground nutmeg
¼ teaspoon salt
¼ teaspoon baking soda

1 cup butter or regular margarine, softened
1 cup light-brown sugar, firmly packed
¼ cup sour cream
½ cup finely chopped blanched almonds

1. Sift together flour, cinnamon, nutmeg, salt, and baking soda; set aside.
2. In large bowl of electric mixer, at medium speed, beat butter, sugar, and sour cream until smooth and fluffy.
3. At low speed, beat in half the flour mixture. With hands, mix in remaining flour mixture and the almonds, to form a stiff dough.
4. Turn out dough onto lightly floured surface. Divide in half. With hands, shape each half into a roll 7 inches long. Wrap each roll in plastic wrap or foil.
5. Refrigerate until firm – about 8 hours, or overnight. (Rolls may be stored in refrigerator a week or 10 days. Bake fresh as desired.)
6. Preheat oven to 375F. With sharp knife, cut as many ⅛-inch slices as desired to bake at one time. Rewrap rest; refrigerate.
7. Place slices, 1 inch apart, on ungreased cookie sheets. Bake 8 to 10 minutes; or until lightly browned.
With spatula, remove to wire rack; cool.
MAKES ABOUT 9 DOZEN IN ALL

BROWN-SUGAR ICEBOX COOKIES

3½ cups sifted all-purpose flour
1 teaspoon baking soda
½ teaspoon salt
1 cup butter or regular margarine, softened
2 cups light-brown sugar, firmly packed

2 eggs
1 teaspoon vanilla extract
1 cup finely chopped walnuts or pecans

1. Sift flour with baking soda and salt; set aside.
2. In large bowl of electric mixer at medium speed, beat butter until light. Gradually beat in sugar. Add eggs and vanilla; continue beating until very light and fluffy.
3. At low speed, beat in half the flour mixture until smooth. Mix in rest, with hands, to form a stiff dough. Add nuts; mix well.
4. Turn out dough onto lightly floured surface. Divide in thirds. With hands, shape each third into a roll 8 inches long.
5. Wrap each in plastic wrap or foil; refrigerate until firm – about 8 hours, or overnight. (Rolls may be stored in refrigerator a week or 10 days. Bake fresh as desired.)
6. Preheat oven to 375F. With sharp knife, cut as many ⅛-inch slices as desired for baking at one time. Rewrap rest of roll; refrigerate.
7. Place slices, 2 inches apart, on ungreased cookie sheets. Bake 7 to 10 minutes, or until lightly browned. Remove to wire rack; cool.
MAKES ABOUT 16 DOZEN IN ALL

VANILLA-NUT ICEBOX COOKIES

2 cups sifted all-purpose flour
1½ teaspoons baking powder
½ teaspoon salt
⅔ cup butter or regular margarine, softened
1 cup sugar
1 egg
1 teaspoon vanilla extract
1 cup finely chopped walnuts, pecans or unsalted peanuts

1. On sheet of waxed paper, sift flour with baking powder and salt; set aside. In large bowl, with wooden spoon, or portable electric mixer at medium speed, beat butter until light. Gradually beat in sugar (photo a). Add egg and vanilla; continue beating until very light and fluffy.
2. At low speed, beat in half the flour mixture; mix in rest, with hands, to form a stiff dough (photo b). Add chopped nuts, mixing to combine well.
3. Turn out dough onto lightly floured surface. Divide in half. With hands, shape each half into a roll 7 inches long (photo c). Wrap each in plastic wrap or foil; refrigerate until firm – about 8 hours, or overnight – before slicing and baking. (Rolls of cookie dough may be stored in refrigerator as long as 10 days. Slice and freshly bake as many as desired.)
4. Preheat oven to 375F. With sharp knife, cut as many ⅛-inch slices as desired for baking at one time (photo d). Rewrap rest of roll; refrigerate. Place slices, 2 inches apart, on ungreased cookie sheets. Bake 8 to 10 minutes, or until lightly browned. With spatula, lift cookies from cookie sheets to wire rack. Let cool completely.
MAKES ABOUT 9 DOZEN IN ALL

Chocolate Nut: Melt 3 squares unsweetened chocolate over hot, not boiling, water. Cool; add to butter mixture. Then proceed, as above.

Lemon Pecan: Omit vanilla; add 1 tablespoon grated lemon peel to creamed butter mixture. Use finely chopped pecans. Proceed as above.

Orange Coconut: Omit vanilla extract; add 1 tablespoon grated orange peel to creamed butter mixture. Omit nuts; use 1 can (3½ oz) flaked coconut, or ½ package (7-oz size) grated coconut. Proceed as above.

PIE SHELL

1. Slice icebox-cookie dough ⅛ inch thick. Press 30 slices, overlapping, in 8-inch pie plate, to form a pie shell.
2. Prick well with fork. Bake at 375F for 10 minutes, or until browned.
3. Let cool in pie plate on wire rack. Fill with a packaged pie-filling mix.

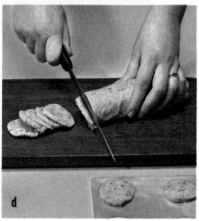

TART SHELLS

1. For each shell, cut 6 slices icebox-cookie dough, 1/8 inch thick. Let stand at room temperature about 10 minutes, to soften.
2. Fit one slice in bottom of ungreased 3-inch muffin-pan cup. Place 5 slices, overlapping, around side. Gently press slices together to conform to pan shape.
3. Prick shell with fork. Bake at 350F for 15 to 20 minutes, or until lightly browned. (If shells puff during baking, prick with fork.)
4. Let cool in pan on wire rack 15 minutes. Carefully lift out of pan. Use as a tart shell for ice cream, sliced fresh strawberries, or a cream filling.

PISTACHIO ICEBOX COOKIES

2 cups sifted all-purpose flour	1/2 teaspoon almond extract
1 1/2 teaspoons baking powder	1/2 cup finely chopped pistachio nuts
1/2 teaspoon salt	Green food color
2/3 cup butter or regular margarine	1 egg white, slightly beaten
1 cup sugar	Chocolate or multicolor nonpareils
1 egg	
1 teaspoon vanilla extract	

1. Sift flour with baking powder and salt; set aside.
2. In large bowl of electric mixer, let butter stand at room temperature until softened. At medium speed, beat butter, sugar, egg and extracts until light and fluffy.
3. At low speed, beat in flour mixture just until well combined.
4. Measure 1 cup batter; turn into small bowl. Add chopped pistachio nuts and 2 or 3 drops food color; mix well. Form into roll 10 inches long; wrap in plastic wrap or foil.
5. Form remaining dough into a 10-by-4 1/2-inch rectangle; wrap. Refrigerate, with pistachio roll, 1 hour.
6. Place pistachio roll lengthwise in center of rectangle of dough. With hands, carefully mold white dough around green roll, covering it completely. Wrap, and refrigerate until very firm – 8 hours or overnight.
7. Preheat oven to 375F. Brush outside of roll with egg white; roll in nonpareils. With sharp knife, cut into 1/8-inch-thick slices. Place, 2 inches apart, on ungreased cookie sheets.
8. Bake 8 to 10 minutes, or until lightly browned. Remove cookies to wire rack; cool completely.
MAKES ABOUT 6 1/2 DOZEN

BUTTERSCOTCH ICEBOX COOKIES

3 1/2 cups sifted all-purpose flour	2 eggs
1 teaspoon baking soda	1 teaspoon vanilla extract
1 cup butter or regular margarine, softened	1 cup chopped salted peanuts
2 cups light-brown sugar, packed	

1. Sift flour with baking soda.
2. In large bowl of electric mixer, at medium speed, beat butter until light. Gradually beat in sugar. Add eggs and vanilla; continue beating until very light and fluffy.
3. At low speed, beat in half of flour mixture until smooth. Mix in rest with hands to form a stiff dough. Add peanuts; mix well.
4. Turn out dough onto lightly floured surface. Divide in thirds. Shape each third into a roll 8 inches long.
5. Wrap each in plastic wrap or foil; refrigerate until firm – about 8 hours or overnight. Or place rolls in freezer for 1 hour, or until firm. (Rolls may be stored in refrigerator a week to ten days, longer in freezer.)
6. Preheat oven to 375F. With sharp knife, cut as many 1/4-inch slices as desired for baking at one time. Rewrap rest of roll; refrigerate.
7. Place slices, 2 inches apart, on ungreased cookie sheets. Bake 8 to 10 minutes, or until lightly browned. Remove to wire rack; cool.
MAKES ABOUT 8 DOZEN

PINWHEEL ICEBOX COOKIES

Filling

1 1/2 cups raisins, chopped	1/2 teaspoon salt
1/4 cup granulated sugar	1/2 teaspoon baking soda
2 tablespoons lemon juice	3/4 cup butter or regular margarine, softened
1/3 cup water	1/2 cup granulated sugar
1/4 cup chopped walnuts	1/2 cup dark-brown sugar, packed
	1 egg, beaten
Cookie Dough	1/2 teaspoon vanilla extract
2 cups unsifted all-purpose flour	

1. Make filling: In small saucepan, combine raisins, 1/4 cup granulated sugar, the lemon juice and 1/3 cup water. Cook, stirring constantly, 5 minutes, or until thickened and liquid has been absorbed. Remove from heat; stir in nuts; cool completely.
2. Make cookie dough: Sift flour with salt and baking soda.
3. In small bowl of electric mixer, at medium speed, cream butter with both kinds of sugar until light and fluffy. Beat in egg and vanilla.

4. At low speed, beat in flour mixture just until combined. Divide dough in half.

5. Roll out dough, one half at a time, between two sheets of waxed paper, to form 11-by-7-inch rectangle. Spread each rectangle with half of filling.

6. From wide end, roll up rectangles tightly. Wrap each in waxed paper; refrigerate 2 hours or overnight. Or place in freezer for 1 hour, or until firm. (Rolls may be stored in refrigerator a week to ten days, longer in freezer. Bake fresh as desired.)

7. Preheat oven to 375F. With sharp knife, slice cookies ¼ inch thick. Arrange, 1 inch apart, on lightly greased cookie sheets. Bake 8 to 10 minutes, or until golden.

MAKES 6 DOZEN

RIBBONS

1 recipe Vanilla-Nut Icebox-Cookie dough, page 7	3 or 4 drops green or red food color (optional)
2 squares unsweetened chocolate, melted	

1. Prepare dough for Vanilla-Nut Icebox Cookies, omitting nuts.

2. Divide evenly into two bowls. Add melted chocolate to one, mixing well. Add food color to other, blending well, or omit, if desired.

3. Turn out dough onto lightly floured surface. Divide chocolate dough into 2 parts and colored dough into 4 parts.

4. With hands, shape each part into a roll 7 inches long. Flatten each roll to uniform width of ½ inches.

5. To assemble one ribbon, stack in order; colored layer, chocolate layer, colored layer. Press lightly, to hold together. Repeat with remaining layers for other ribbon.

6. Wrap each in waxed paper or foil; refrigerate until firm – several hours, or overnight.

7. Slice and bake as directed for Vanilla-Nut Icebox Cookies.

MAKES ABOUT 8 DOZEN

CINNAMON ICEBOX COOKIES

3 cups sifted all-purpose flour	1 cup granulated sugar
½ teaspoon baking powder	½ cup light-brown sugar, firmly packed
½ teaspoon baking soda	½ cup buttermilk or sour milk*
¼ teaspoon salt	1 cup finely chopped pecans or unblanched almonds
1 tablespoon ground cinnamon	
½ cup butter or regular margarine, softened	

1. Sift flour with baking powder, baking soda, salt, and cinnamon; set aside.

2. In large bowl, with wooden spoon, or portable electric mixer at medium speed, beat butter until light. Gradually beat in sugars until light and fluffy.

3. At low speed, beat in buttermilk until smooth.

4. Gradually beat in half of flour mixture. Mix in rest, with hands, to form a stiff dough. Add nuts, mixing to combine well.

5. On lightly floured surface, divide dough in half. With hands, shape each half into a roll 7 inches long.

6. Wrap each roll in plastic wrap or foil; refrigerate until firm – about 8 hours, or overnight – before slicing and baking. (Rolls may be stored in refrigerator a week or 10 days. Bake fresh as desired.)

7. Preheat oven to 375F. With a sharp knife, cut as many ⅛-inch slices as desired for baking at one time. Then rewrap rest of roll, and refrigerate.

8. Place slices, 2 inches apart, on ungreased cookie sheets. Bake 8 to 10 minutes, or until golden. Remove to wire rack; cool.

MAKES ABOUT 9 DOZEN IN ALL

*To sour milk: Place ½ teaspoons vinegar or lemon juice in a measuring cup. Add milk to measure ½ cup. Let stand a few minutes.

OATMEAL ICEBOX COOKIES

1 cup sifted all-purpose flour	½ cup granulated sugar
½ teaspoon baking soda	½ cup light-brown sugar, firmly packed
½ teaspoon salt	1 egg
½ teaspoon ground cinnamon	2 tablespoons honey
½ cup butter or regular margarine, softened	1½ cups rolled oats

1. Sift flour with baking soda, salt, and cinnamon; set aside.

2. In large bowl, with wooden spoon, or portable electric mixer at medium speed, beat butter until light. Gradually beat in sugars. Add egg and honey; continue beating until very light and fluffy.

3. At low speed, gradually add half the flour mixture. Mix in rest, with hands, to form a stiff dough.

4. Add oats, mixing to combine well. Refrigerate 30 minutes.

5. Divide dough in half. On lightly floured surface, shape each half into a roll 7 inches long. Wrap in plastic wrap or foil; refrigerate until firm – about 8 hours, or overnight. (Rolls may be stored in refrigerator a week or 10 days. Bake fresh as desired.)

6. Preheat oven to 375F. With sharp knife, cut as many ⅛-inch slices as desired for baking at one time. Rewrap rest of roll; refrigerate.

7. Place slices, 2 inches apart, on ungreased cookie sheets. Bake 8 to 10 minutes, or until lightly browned. Remove to wire rack; cool.

MAKES ABOUT 7 DOZEN IN ALL

SPICE ICEBOX COOKIES

4 cups sifted all-purpose flour
1 teaspoon baking soda
½ teaspoon salt
1 tablespoon pumpkin-pie spice
1 cup butter or regular margarine, softened
1 cup sugar
¼ cup dark corn syrup
½ cup sour cream

1. Sift flour with baking soda, salt, and pumpkin-pie spice; set aside.
2. In large bowl, with wooden spoon, or portable electric mixer at medium speed, beat butter until light. Gradually beat in sugar until light and fluffy.
3. At low speed, beat in corn syrup and sour cream until smooth.
4. Gradually beat in half of flour mixture. Mix in rest, with hands, to form a stiff dough.
5. Turn out dough onto lightly floured surface. Divide into thirds. With hands, shape each third into a roll 7 inches long.
6. Wrap each in plastic wrap or foil; refrigerate until firm – about 8 hours, or overnight – before baking. (Rolls may be stored in refrigerator a week or 10 days. Bake fresh as desired.)
7. Preheat oven to 375F. Lightly grease cookie sheets.
8. With sharp knife, cut as many ⅛-inch slices as desired for baking at one time. Rewrap rest of roll; refrigerate.
9. Place slices, 2 inches apart, on prepared cookie sheets. Bake 8 to 10 minutes, or until golden-brown. Remove to wire rack; cool.
MAKES ABOUT 14 DOZEN IN ALL

CHOCOLATE-OATMEAL REFRIGERATOR COOKIES

1 cup sifted all-purpose flour
1 teaspoon baking powder
½ teaspoon salt
1 cup butter or regular margarine, softened
1 cup sugar
1 egg
1 tablespoon vanilla extract
1 cup uncooked quick-cooking oats
1 pkg (6 oz) semisweet-chocolate pieces, finely chopped

1. Sift flour with baking powder and salt; set aside.
2. In large bowl, with wooden spoon, or portable electric mixer at medium speed, cream butter with sugar until light and fluffy.
3. Stir in egg and vanilla until smooth.
4. Add flour mixture, stirring until well combined. Stir in oats and chocolate; mix well.
5. Turn dough onto lightly floured surface. Divide in half.
6. With hands, shape each half into a roll 10 inches long and 1½ inches in diameter. (If dough is too soft to shape, refrigerate 30 minutes.)

7. Wrap each roll in waxed paper or foil; refrigerate until firm – several hours or overnight.
8. Preheat oven to 375F. With sharp knife, cut each roll into slices ¼ inch thick.
9. Place slices, 2 inches apart, on ungreased cookie sheets. Bake 10 to 12 minutes, or until golden.
10. Remove to wire rack; cool.
MAKES ABOUT 6½ DOZEN

PEANUT-BUTTER PINWHEELS
(pictured on pages 36-37)

2½ cups sifted all-purpose flour
1 teaspoon baking soda
½ teaspoon salt
¾ cup butter or regular margarine, softened
1 cup light-brown sugar, firmly packed
1 cup chunk-style peanut butter

1 egg
1 teaspoon vanilla extract

Filling
1 pkg (6 oz) semisweet chocolate pieces
1 teaspoon butter or margarine

1. Sift flour with baking soda and salt; set aside.
2. In large bowl, with wooden spoon, or portable electric mixer at medium speed, beat butter until light. Gradually beat in sugar, beating until light and fluffy.
3. Add peanut butter, egg, and vanilla; beat until smooth.
4. At low speed, gradually add half of flour mixture. Mix in rest, with hands, to form a stiff dough. Refrigerate 30 minutes.
5. Meanwhile, make Filling: Melt chocolate pieces over hot, not boiling, water. Stir in butter. Let cool completely.
6. Divide dough in half. Between 2 pieces waxed paper, roll each into an 8-by-10-inch rectangle. Remove top sheet of waxed paper. Spread each rectangle with half the chocolate mixture.
7. From long side, roll each tightly, jelly-roll fashion; remove bottom sheet of waxed paper as you roll. Gently press edge, to seal.
8. Wrap separately, seam side down, in plastic wrap or foil. Refrigerate until firm – about 8 hours, or overnight – before slicing and baking. (Rolls may be stored in refrigerator a week or 10 days. Bake fresh as needed.)
9. Preheat oven to 375F. Lightly grease cookie sheets.
10. With sharp knife, cut as many ¼-inch slices as desired for baking at one time. Rewrap rest of roll; refrigerate.
11. Place slices, 1½ inches apart, on prepared cookie sheets. Bake about 8 minutes, or until lightly browned. Remove to wire rack; cool.
MAKES ABOUT 5 DOZEN IN ALL

DATE-NUT PINWHEELS

2 cups sifted all-purpose flour
1½ teaspoons baking powder
½ teaspoon salt
1 teaspoon ground cinnamon
½ teaspoon ground ginger
½ teaspoon ground nutmeg
⅔ cup butter or regular margarine, softened
1 cup sugar

1 egg
1 teaspoon vanilla extract

Date-Nut Filling
1 pkg (8 oz) pitted dates, cut up
½ cup sugar
½ cup water
2 teaspoons grated lemon peel
½ cup finely chopped walnuts

1. Sift flour with baking powder, salt, cinnamon, ginger, and nutmeg; set aside.
2. In large bowl, with wooden spoon, or portable electric mixer at medium speed, beat butter until light. Gradually beat in sugar. Add egg and vanilla; continue beating until very light and fluffy.
3. At low speed, gradually add half of flour mixture. Mix in rest, with hands, to form a stiff dough. Refrigerate 1 hour.
4. Meanwhile, make Date-Nut Filling: In small saucepan, combine dates and sugar with ½ cup water. Cook, stirring, over medium heat, until mixture thickens – about 5 minutes. Remove from heat. Stir in lemon peel and nuts. Cool completely.
5. Divide dough in half. On a lightly floured surface, roll each half into an 8-by-10-inch rectangle. Spread each rectangle with half the date-nut mixture.
6. From long side, roll each, jelly-roll fashion. Gently press edge, to seal.
7. Wrap separately, seam side down, in plastic wrap or foil. Refrigerate until firm – about 8 hours, or overnight – before baking. (Rolls may be stored in refrigerator a week or 10 days. Bake fresh as needed.)
8. Preheat oven to 375F. Lightly grease cookie sheets.
9. With sharp knife, cut as many ⅛-inch slices as desired for baking at one time. Rewrap rest of roll; refrigerate.

10. Place slices, 2 inches apart, on prepared cookie sheets. Bake 8 to 10 minutes, or until lightly browned. Let stand 1 minute. Remove to wire rack; cool.

MAKES ABOUT 9 DOZEN IN ALL

ORANGE-FIG PINWHEELS: In small saucepan, combine 1¼ cups finely chopped figs and ¼ cup sugar with ¾ cup water. Cook, stirring, over medium heat until mixture is thickened – about 10 minutes. Remove from heat. Stir in 1 tablespoon grated orange peel and ½ cup finely chopped walnuts. Cool completely. Make cookies as directed above, substituting orange-fig filling.

PETTICOAT TAILS

2½ cups sifted all-purpose flour
½ teaspoon baking soda
¼ teaspoon salt
1½ cups butter, softened

1½ cups sifted confectioners' sugar
1 teaspoon vanilla extract or rose water

1. Sift flour with baking soda and salt; set aside.
2. In large bowl, with wooden spoon, or portable electric mixer at medium speed, beat butter, sugar, and vanilla until light and fluffy.
3. Add flour mixture; mix well, with hands, to make a soft dough. Refrigerate 30 minutes.
4. Turn out dough onto lightly floured surface. Divide in half. With hands, shape each into a roll 8 inches long.
5. Wrap each in waxed paper or foil; refrigerate until firm – several hours, or overnight – before baking. (Rolls may be stored in refrigerator a week or 10 days; bake fresh as needed.)
6. Preheat oven to 375F. With sharp knife, cut as many ⅛-inch slices as desired for one baking. Rewrap roll; refrigerate.
7. Place slices, 1 inch apart, on ungreased cookie sheets. Bake 8 to 10 minutes, or until lightly browned. Let stand 1 minute. Remove to wire rack; cool.

MAKES ABOUT 8 DOZEN IN ALL

Peanut-Butter Drops
Crunch Drops
Ginger Drops
Raisin-Spice Drops
Toasted Oatmeal Cookies
Double-Chocolate Drops
Pecan Drops

DROP

COOKIES are made from a soft dough and dropped from the spoon directly onto the cookie sheet. Actually, "dropped" is a little misleading, as the mixture must be stiff enough to be pushed from the spoon. Drop cookies can be soft, with a cake-like texture; crisp; or even brittle. Their shape is irregular, as they spread on the cookie sheet. You can make them in a wide variety of delicious flavors. A kitchen teaspoon, not a measuring spoon, is used for dropping the correct amount of cookie dough onto the prepared cookie sheet. Place waxed paper under wire rack for cookies that are to be glazed, to catch any drippings.

APPLE DROP COOKIES

2 cups sifted all-purpose flour
1 teaspoon baking soda
½ teaspoon salt
1 teaspoon ground cinnamon
½ teaspoon ground cloves
½ teaspoon ground allspice
½ teaspoon ground nutmeg
1 cup finely chopped walnuts
1 cup finely chopped unpared red apple (1 small apple)
1 cup raisins, chopped
½ cup butter or regular margarine, softened
1⅓ cups light-brown sugar, firmly packed
1 egg, unbeaten
¼ cup apple juice or cider

1. Preheat oven to 400F. Lightly grease cookie sheets.
2. Sift flour with baking soda, salt, and spices into large bowl. Stir in walnuts, apple, and raisins; set aside.
3. In large bowl of electric mixer, at medium speed, cream butter and sugar until light and fluffy.
4. Add egg and apple juice; beat until combined.
5. Stir in flour mixture; mix well.
6. Drop by tablespoonfuls, 2 inches apart, onto prepared cookie sheets.
7. Bake 8 minutes, or until golden-brown.
MAKES ABOUT 4 DOZEN

ORANGE-GLAZED BANANA COOKIES

2½ cups sifted all-purpose flour
2 teaspoons baking powder
¼ teaspoon baking soda
½ teaspoon salt
½ teaspoon ground cinnamon
¼ teaspoon ground cloves
½ cup butter or regular margarine, softened
1 cup light-brown sugar, firmly packed
2 eggs
1 cup mashed ripe bananas (about 3)
1 teaspoon vanilla extract
½ cup coarsely chopped walnuts

Orange Glaze
3 cups sifted confectioners' sugar
1 tablespoon grated orange peel
3 to 4 tablespoons milk

1. Preheat oven to 400F. Lightly grease cookie sheets.
2. Sift flour with baking powder, baking soda, salt, cinnamon, and cloves; set aside.
3. In large bowl of electric mixer, at medium speed, beat butter, sugar, and eggs until light and fluffy.
4. Beat in bananas and vanilla until smooth.
5. Gradually beat in flour mixture until well combined. Stir in nuts.

6. Drop by rounded teaspoonfuls, 2 inches apart, onto prepared cookie sheets.
7. Bake 12 to 15 minutes, or until golden-brown. Remove to wire rack; cool partially.
8. Meanwhile, make Glaze: In a medium bowl, combine sugar, orange peel, and milk; stir until smooth.
9. Spread top of slightly warm cookies with glaze.
MAKES ABOUT 4½ DOZEN

BANANA-OATMEAL COOKIES

1½ cups sifted all-purpose flour
1 teaspoon salt
½ teaspoon baking soda
½ teaspoon ground nutmeg
¾ teaspoon ground cinnamon
¾ cup butter or regular margarine, softened
1 cup sugar
1 egg
1 cup mashed ripe bananas (about 3)
1 teaspoon vanilla extract
1½ cups raw quick-cooking oats
½ cup coarsely chopped walnuts

1. Sift flour with salt, baking soda, nutmeg, and cinnamon; set aside.
2. In large bowl, with wooden spoon or portable electric mixer at medium speed, beat butter, sugar, and egg until light and fluffy.
3. Beat in bananas and vanilla until smooth.
4. Gradually stir in flour mixture and oats until well combined. Stir in nuts. Refrigerate 30 minutes.
5. Meanwhile, preheat oven to 400F. Lightly grease cookie sheets.
6. Drop batter by rounded teaspoonfuls, 2 inches apart, onto prepared cookie sheets.
7. Bake 12 to 15 minutes, or until golden. Remove to wire rack; cool.
MAKES ABOUT 3½ DOZEN

BRAZIL-NUT COOKIES
(pictured on pages 36-37)

1¾ cups sifted all-purpose flour
½ teaspoon salt
1 cup butter or regular margarine, softened
1 cup granulated sugar
1 egg
1 teaspoon vanilla extract
1½ cups ground or finely chopped Brazil nuts

1. Sift flour with salt; set aside.
2. In large bowl, with wooden spoon, or portable electric mixer at medium speed, beat butter, sugar, egg, and vanilla until light and fluffy.
3. Add Brazil nuts; stir until well blended.
4. Gradually beat in flour mixture until well combined. Refrigerate 30 minutes.
5. Meanwhile, preheat oven to 400F. Lightly grease cookie sheets.

CHOCOLATE-CHIP COOKIES

1 cup plus 2 tablespoons
  sifted all-purpose flour
1/2 teaspoon baking soda
1/2 teaspoon salt
1/2 cup granulated sugar
1/4 cup light-brown sugar,
  firmly packed
1 egg

1 teaspoon vanilla
  extract
1/2 cup butter or regular
  margarine, softened
1/2 cup coarsely chopped
  walnuts or pecans
1 pkg (6 oz) semisweet-
  chocolate pieces

1. Preheat oven to 375F.
2. Into large bowl, sift flour with baking soda and salt.
3. Add sugars, egg, vanilla, and butter. With wooden spoon, or portable electric mixer at medium speed, beat until smooth and well combined – about 1 minute.
4. Stir in nuts and chocolate pieces.
5. Drop by teaspoonfuls, 2 inches apart, onto ungreased cookie sheets.
6. Bake 10 to 12 minutes, or until golden. Remove to wire rack; cool.
MAKES ABOUT 4 DOZEN

CHOCOLATE-MALTED COOKIES

1 1/4 cups sifted all-
  purpose flour
1 cup instant sweetened
  chocolate-flavored
  malted-milk powder
1 teaspoon baking
  powder
1/4 teaspoon salt
1/2 cup butter or regular
  margarine, softened

1 cup light-brown sugar,
  firmly packed
1 egg
1 teaspoon vanilla
  extract
1/4 cup undiluted
  evaporated milk
1 cup coarsely chopped
  walnuts

1. Sift together flour, malted-milk powder, baking powder, and salt; set aside.
2. In large bowl, with portable electric mixer at medium speed, or wooden spoon, beat butter, sugar, egg, and vanilla until fluffy. Beat in milk until smooth.
3. Gradually stir in flour mixture, mixing until well combined. Stir in nuts.
4. Refrigerate, covered, at least 1 hour.
5. Preheat oven to 350F. Lightly grease cookie sheets.
6. Drop batter by rounded teaspoonfuls, 2 inches apart, onto prepared cookie sheets. Bake 10 to 12 minutes, or until set but not brown.
7. Remove to wire rack; cool completely.
MAKES ABOUT 4 1/2 DOZEN

6. Drop by slightly rounded teaspoonfuls, 2 inches apart, onto prepared cookie sheets. Decorate, if desired, with strips of angelica or citron.
7. Bake 8 to 10 minutes, or until golden-brown around the edges. Remove to wire rack; cool.
MAKES ABOUT 5 DOZEN

GLAZED BRAZIL-NUT COOKIES: Add 1 cup Brazil nuts to batter; reserve 1/2 cup for topping. Make Glaze: In medium bowl, with wooden spoon, beat 3 cups sifted confectioners' sugar, 1/4 cup light cream, and 1 teaspoon vanilla extract until smooth. Add 2 squares unsweetened chocolate, melted; mix well. Spread tops of slightly warm cookies with glaze. Sprinkle with remaining nuts.

DOUBLE-CHOCOLATE DROPS
(pictured on pages 12-13)

1 pkg (6 oz) semisweet-
  chocolate pieces
1 cup sifted all-purpose
  flour
1/2 teaspoon baking soda
1/2 teaspoon salt
1/2 cup butter or regular
  margarine, softened

1/2 cup sugar
1 egg
1/4 cup warm water
1/2 cup coarsely chopped
  walnuts or pecans

1. In top of double boiler, over hot, not boiling, water, melt 1/2 cup chocolate pieces. Let cool.
2. Sift together flour, baking soda, and salt; set aside.
3. In large bowl of electric mixer, at medium speed, beat butter, sugar, and egg until light and fluffy.
4. At low speed, beat in melted chocolate and 1/4 cup warm water.
5. Then beat in flour mixture, just until combined.
6. With spoon, stir in remaining chocolate pieces and the nuts. Refrigerate 30 minutes.
7. Meanwhile, preheat oven to 375F. Lightly grease cookie sheets.
8. Drop batter by teaspoonfuls, 3 inches apart, onto prepared cookie sheets. Decorate, if desired, with chopped nuts.
9. Bake 10 to 12 minutes. Remove to wire rack; cool.
MAKES ABOUT 3 DOZEN

GLAZED FUDGE DROPS

1¾ cups sifted all-purpose flour
2 teaspoons baking powder
½ teaspoon salt
¼ cup sifted unsweetened cocoa
2 eggs
⅔ cup salad oil
1 teaspoon vanilla extract
¼ teaspoon almond extract

1 cup granulated sugar
1 cup coarsely chopped walnuts

Glaze
2 cups sifted confectioners' sugar
2 to 3 tablespoons milk

Chocolate nonpareils

1. Sift flour with baking powder, salt, and cocoa; set aside.
2. In medium bowl, beat eggs slightly. Stir in salad oil, extracts, and sugar until thoroughly combined.
3. With wooden spoon, beat in flour mixture until smooth. Stir in nuts. Refrigerate 30 minutes.
4. Meanwhile, preheat oven to 400F. Drop batter by slightly rounded teaspoonfuls, 2 inches apart, onto ungreased cookie sheets.
5. Bake 8 to 10 minutes. Remove to wire rack; cool partially.
6. Make Glaze: In medium bowl, combine sugar and milk; stir until smooth.
7. Spread top of slightly warm cookies with glaze. Sprinkle with nonpareils.
MAKES ABOUT 3½ DOZEN

CRISP COCOA COOKIES

1¼ cups sifted all-purpose flour
½ teaspoon baking soda
¼ teaspoon salt
½ cup butter or regular margarine, softened
1 cup sugar

1 egg
1 teaspoon vanilla extract
1 cup cocoa-flavored, sweetened crisp rice cereal

1. Preheat oven to 350F. Lightly grease cookie sheets.
2. Sift flour with baking soda and salt; set aside.
3. In large bowl, with wooden spoon, or portable electric mixer at medium speed, cream butter with sugar until light and fluffy. Beat in egg and vanilla until smooth.
4. Stir in flour mixture and cereal; mix well.
5. Drop by teaspoonfuls, 2 inches apart, onto prepared cookie sheets. Bake about 12 minutes.
6. Remove to wire rack; cool.
MAKES ABOUT 4 DOZEN

GLAZED CHOCOLATE COOKIES

1¼ cups sifted all-purpose flour
¼ teaspoon salt
¼ teaspoon baking soda
½ cup butter or regular margarine, softened
1 cup light-brown sugar, firmly packed
1 egg
1 teaspoon vanilla
2 envelopes (1-oz size) no-melt unsweetened chocolate

½ cup buttermilk
1 cup coarsely chopped walnuts or pecans

Glaze
2½ cups sifted confectioners' sugar
¼ cup light cream
1 teaspoon vanilla extract
1 envelope (1 oz) no-melt unsweetened chocolate

1. Preheat oven to 375F. Sift together flour, salt, and baking soda; set aside.
2. In large bowl of electric mixer, at medium speed, beat butter, sugar, egg, and vanilla until light and fluffy.
3. Beat in chocolate.
4. At low speed, beat in flour mixture alternately with buttermilk until well combined.
5. Stir in nuts. Mixture will be soft.
6. Drop by slightly rounded teaspoonfuls, 2 inches apart, onto ungreased cookie sheets.
7. Bake 8 to 10 minutes. Remove to wire rack; cool partially.
8. Meanwhile, make Glaze: In a medium bowl, combine sugar, cream, and vanilla. With spoon, beat until smooth. Add chocolate; mix well. (If glaze is too stiff to spread easily, add a little more cream.)
9. Glaze tops of warm cookies.
MAKES ABOUT 4 DOZEN

COCONUT-ALMOND DROPS

¾ cup sweetened condensed milk
2 cans (3½-oz size) flaked coconut
1 teaspoon vanilla extract

½ teaspoon almond extract
1 cup toasted slivered almonds

1. Preheat oven to 300F. Lighlty grease cookie sheets.
2. In medium bowl, combine condensed milk with remaining ingredients, stirring gently until well mixed.
3. Drop by teaspoonfuls, 1 inch apart, onto prepared cookie sheets.
4. Bake about 12 minutes, or until light-golden. Cool on wire rack.
MAKES ABOUT 4 DOZEN

FILBERT-CHOCOLATE DROPS

2 cups sifted all-purpose
  flour
1 teaspoon baking
  powder
1/2 cup sifted
  unsweetened cocoa
1/2 teaspoon salt
1 tablespoon vinegar
3/4 cup plus 3 tablespoons
  milk
1 teaspoon baking soda
2/3 cup butter or regular
  margarine, softened
1 cup granulated sugar
1 egg

1 1/2 teaspoons vanilla
  extract
1 cup finely chopped
  filberts
Frosting
2 1/2 tablespoons butter or
  regular margarine,
  softened
1 1/4 cups sifted
  confectioners' sugar
3 tablespoons sifted
  unsweetened cocoa
1/4 teaspoon salt
3/4 cup chopped filberts

1. Preheat oven to 325F. Sift flour with baking powder, cocoa, and salt; set aside.
2. Combine vinegar, milk, and baking soda in measuring cup.
3. In large bowl of electric mixer, at medium speed, beat butter until light.
4. Gradually add sugar, beating until very light and fluffy. Beat in egg and vanilla.
5. At low speed, gradually blend in flour mixture alternately with milk mixture just until blended. Stir in 1 cup chopped filberts.
6. Drop by rounded teaspoonfuls, 1 inch apart, onto ungreased cookie sheets. Bake 10 minutes. Remove to wire rack; cool.
7. Meanwhile, make Frosting: Cream butter, with spoon, in small bowl.
8. Combine sugar, cocoa, and salt. Gradually add to butter alternately with 2 1/2 tablespoons hot water, stirring until smooth.
9. Frost cookies. Top with chopped filberts.
MAKES ABOUT 6 1/2 DOZEN

COCONUT KISSES

2 egg whites
1/2 cup sifted
  confectioners' sugar

1/4 teaspoon lemon
  extract
1 can (3 1/2 oz) flaked
  coconut

1. Preheat oven to 300F. Line cookie sheet with greased brown paper.
2. In small bowl of electric mixer, at high speed, beat egg whites just until soft peaks form when beater is slowly raised. Beat in sugar in thirds, beating until stiff peaks are formed when beater is slowly raised.
3. Fold in lemon extract and coconut until well blended.
4. Drop by rounded teaspoonfuls, 1 inch apart, onto prepared cookie sheets. Bake 30 to 35 minutes, or until light-golden.

5. Remove from paper at once; let cool completely on a wire rack.
MAKES ABOUT 12

COCONUT MACAROONS

3 egg whites, beaten
  until stiff
1 cup sugar
1 tablespoon cornstarch
1/4 teaspoon salt

2 cups packaged flaked
  coconut
1/2 teaspoon almond
  extract

1. Preheat oven to 300F. Lightly grease cookie sheets.
2. In top of double boiler, combine egg whites, sugar, and cornstarch. Cook over boiling water, stirring constantly, 20 minutes.
3. Remove from heat. Add salt, coconut, and almond extract, stirring until well combined.
4. Drop by teaspoonfuls 1/2 inch apart, onto prepared cookie sheets. Bake 18 to 20 minutes, or until lightly browned. Remove to wire rack; cool.
MAKES ABOUT 2 DOZEN

COCONUT CRISPS

2 cups sifted all-purpose
  flour
1 teaspoon baking
  powder
1 teaspoon baking soda
1/2 teaspoon salt
1 cup uncooked rolled
  oats
1 can (3 1/2 oz) flaked
  coconut

3/4 cup shortening
3/4 cup granulated sugar
1/2 cup light-brown sugar,
  firmly packed
1 teaspoon vanilla
  extract
1 egg, beaten

1. Preheat oven to 375F. Lightly grease cookie sheets.
2. Into large bowl, sift flour with baking powder, baking soda, and salt. Add rolled oats and coconut; set aside.
3. In large bowl of electric mixer at medium speed, cream shortening with sugars until light and fluffy. Beat in vanilla and egg.
4. At low speed, gradually add flour mixture, to make a stiff dough.
5. Drop by teaspoonfuls, 1 inch apart, onto prepared cookie sheets. Bake 10 minutes, or until light-golden. Let cool on cookie sheets 5 minutes; then remove to wire rack; cool.
MAKES ABOUT 5 DOZEN

CRUNCH DROPS
(pictured on pages 12-13)

2 cups sifted all-purpose flour	1 cup granulated sugar
1 teaspoon baking soda	2 eggs
½ teaspoon salt	1 teaspoon vanilla extract
1 cup butter or regular margarine, softened	2 cups uncooked quick-cooking oats
1 cup light-brown sugar, firmly packed	1 can (3½ oz) flaked coconut

1. Preheat oven to 375F. Lightly grease cookie sheets.
2. Sift flour with baking soda and salt; set aside.
3. In large bowl of electric mixer, at medium speed, beat butter, sugars, eggs, and vanilla until light and fluffy.
4. At low speed, beat in flour mixture until well combined.
5. Stir in oats and coconut until well blended, to make a stiff dough.
6. Drop by slightly rounded teaspoonfuls, 2 inches apart, onto prepared cookie sheets.
7. Bake 12 to 15 minutes. Remove to wire rack; cool.
MAKES ABOUT 5 DOZEN

DATE ROCKS

2½ cups sifted all-purpose flour	1 cup sugar
¾ teaspoon baking soda	3 eggs
½ teaspoon salt	1 teaspoon vanilla extract
1 teaspoon ground cinnamon	1 pkg (8 oz) pitted dates, coarsely chopped
½ teaspoon ground cloves	1 cup coarsely chopped walnuts or pecans
1 cup butter or regular margarine, softened	

1. Sift together flour, baking soda, salt, cinnamon, and cloves; set aside.
2. In large bowl of electric mixer, at medium speed, beat butter, sugar, eggs, and vanilla until smooth and fluffy.
3. With wooden spoon, stir in flour mixture until well combined. Then stir in dates and walnuts. Dough will be stiff.
4. Refrigerate, covered, at least 1 hour.
5. Preheat oven to 400F. Lightly grease cookie sheets.
6. Drop dough by rounded teaspoonfuls, 2 inches apart, onto prepared cookie sheets.
7. Bake 8 to 10 minutes, or until lightly browned. Remove to wire rack; cool completely.
MAKES ABOUT 6 DOZEN

COFFEE DROP COOKIES

½ cup butter or regular margarine, softened	½ cup chopped walnuts
½ cup granulated sugar	**Glaze**
1 egg	2¼ cups sifted confectioners' sugar
2 tablespoons instant coffee	¼ cup cold coffee
2 tablespoons hot water	3 tablespoons butter or margarine, melted
1½ cups sifted all-purpose flour	1 tablespoon unsweetened cocoa
¼ cup milk	

1. Preheat oven to 375F. Lightly grease cookie sheets.
2. In medium bowl, with portable electric mixer at medium speed, beat butter with sugar until light.
3. Add egg; beat until light and fluffy.
4. Dissolve instant coffee in 2 tablespoons hot water. Stir into butter mixture.
5. Beat in flour and milk alternately. Stir in chopped nuts.
6. Drop, by heaping teaspoonfuls, 2 inches apart, onto prepared cookie sheets. Bake 8 to 10 minutes, or until lightly browned. Let cool on wire rack.
7. Meanwhile, make Glaze: In small bowl, add sugar and coffee alternately to butter, stirring until smooth. Stir in cocoa.
8. Spread on cookies; let harden before serving.
MAKES ABOUT 3 DOZEN

FRUITCAKE COOKIES

2½ cups sifted all-purpose flour
1 teaspoon baking soda
1 teaspoon salt
1 teaspoon ground cinnamon
1 cup butter or regular margarine, softened
1½ cups sugar
2 eggs
4 pkg (8-oz size) pitted dates, coarsely chopped

2 jars (4-oz size) cubed candied pineapple, finely chopped
1 cup candied cherries, quartered
1 can (3½ oz) toasted sliced almonds, coarsely chopped
1 cup toasted Brazil nuts, coarsely chopped

1. Preheat oven to 400F. Sift flour with baking soda, salt, and cinnamon; set aside.
2. In large bowl, with wooden spoon, or portable electric mixer at medium speed, beat butter, sugar, and eggs until light and fluffy.
3. Stir in flour mixture until well combined. Add fruits and nuts, mixing well.
4. Drop by level tablespoonfuls*, 2 inches apart, onto ungreased cookie sheets.
5. Bake 8 to 10 minutes, or until golden-brown. Let stand 1 minute. Remove to wire rack; cool.
*Use a measuring tablespoon.
MAKES ABOUT 8 DOZEN

GLAZED GINGER COOKIES

2½ cups sifted all-purpose flour
½ teaspoon salt
1 teaspoon baking powder
¼ teaspoon baking soda
1 teaspoon ground cinnamon
½ teaspoon ground cloves
1 teaspoon ground ginger
½ cup shortening

½ cup light-brown sugar, firmly packed
1 egg
½ cup light molasses
1 tablespoon vinegar
½ cup water
½ cup seedless raisins (optional)

Glaze
2 cups sifted confectioners' sugar
2 to 3 tablespoons milk

1. Sift flour with salt, baking powder, baking soda, cinnamon, cloves, and ginger; set aside.
2. In large bowl, with wooden spoon, or portable electric mixer at medium speed, beat shortening, sugar, and egg until light and fluffy.
3. Stir in molasses, vinegar, and ½ cup water. Mixture will look curdled.

4. Gradually stir in the flour mixture until smooth. Stir in raisins. Refrigerate 30 minutes.
5. Meanwhile, preheat oven to 375F. Lightly grease cookie sheets.
6. Drop by slightly rounded teaspoonfuls, 2 inches apart, onto prepared cookie sheets.
7. Bake 10 to 12 minutes, or until set. Remove to wire rack; cool partially.
8. Make Glaze: In medium bowl, combine sugar and milk; stir until smooth.
9. Spread tops of cookies with glaze while still slightly warm. Decorate, if desired, with additional raisins.
MAKES ABOUT 4 DOZEN

HONEY-GINGER DROPS

3 cups sifted all-purpose flour
¼ teaspoon salt
2 teaspoons baking powder
2 teaspoons ground ginger

1 cup shortening
1 cup sugar
1 egg
1 cup honey
1 cup coarsely chopped walnuts or pecans

1. Preheat oven to 375F. Lightly grease cookie sheets.
2. Sift flour with salt, baking powder, and ginger; set aside.
3. In large bowl, with portable electric mixer at medium speed, beat shortening, sugar, and egg until smooth and fluffy. Add honey; beat until combined.
4. With wooden spoon, stir in flour mixture, blending well. Stir in nuts.
5. Drop by rounded teaspoonfuls, 2 inches apart, onto prepared cookie sheets. Decorate each, if desired, with walnut half.
6. Bake 10 to 12 minutes, or until lightly browned.
7. Remove to wire rack; cool completely.
MAKES ABOUT 4 DOZEN

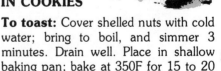

HOW TO USE NUTS IN COOKIES

To toast: Cover shelled nuts with cold water; bring to boil, and simmer 3 minutes. Drain well. Place in shallow baking pan; bake at 350F for 15 to 20 minutes, or until they are golden.

To chop: Spread shelled nuts on wooden board. Hold tip of French knife against board with left hand; with right hand, move handle up and down across nuts (or chop in food processor or blender).

GINGER DROPS
(pictured on pages 12-13)

3 cups sifted all-purpose flour
2 teaspoons baking soda
2 teaspoons ground cinnamon
1 teaspoon ground cloves
2 tablespoons ground ginger
¾ cup butter or regular margarine, softened
¾ cup shortening
2 cups sugar
2 eggs
½ cup light molasses

1. Preheat oven to 375F.
2. Sift flour with baking soda, cinnamon, cloves, and ginger; set aside.
3. In large bowl of electric mixer, at medium speed, beat butter, shortening, sugar, and eggs until light and fluffy. Add molasses; beat until thoroughly combined. At low speed, beat in flour mixture until well combined.
4. Drop by teaspoonfuls, 3 inches apart, onto ungreased cookie sheets. Bake 10 to 12 minutes. Remove to wire rack; cool.
MAKES ABOUT 7 DOZEN

MOLASSES-PRUNE DROPS

1 cup dried prunes (about 16)
1⅓ cups sifted all-purpose flour
2 teaspoons baking powder
⅛ teaspoon baking soda
⅛ teaspoon salt
¼ teaspoon ground ginger
¼ teaspoon ground cinnamon
¼ cup butter or regular margarine, softened, or shortening
¼ cup light-brown sugar, firmly packed
¼ cup granulated sugar
1 egg
2 tablespoons molasses
3 tablespoons milk
¼ cup walnuts, coarsely chopped

1. In small saucepan, combine prunes and 1¾ cups water. Over medium heat, cook, uncovered, 30 minutes. Drain; remove pits; with scissors, cut prunes into eighths.
2. Meanwhile, preheat oven to 350F. Lightly grease cookie sheets.
3. Sift flour with baking powder, baking soda, salt, ginger, and cinnamon; set aside.
4. In large bowl of electric mixer, at medium speed, cream butter with sugars until light. Add egg, molasses, and milk; beat until light and fluffy.
5. At low speed, beat in flour mixture until well combined. Stir in walnuts and prunes.
6. Drop by teaspoonfuls, 2 inches apart, onto prepared cookie sheets. Bake 15 minutes, or until golden-brown. Let cool about 5 minutes on cookie sheets; remove to wire rack; cool.
MAKES ABOUT 4 DOZEN

HERMITS

3½ cups sifted all-purpose flour
1 teaspoon baking soda
1 teaspoon salt
1 teaspoon ground nutmeg
1 teaspoon ground cinnamon
1 cup butter or regular margarine, softened
2 cups light-brown sugar, firmly packed
2 eggs
½ cup cold black coffee
1¾ cups seedless raisins
1¾ cups chopped dried apricots

1. Sift together flour, baking soda, salt, and spices; set aside.
2. In large bowl of electric mixer, at medium speed, cream butter with sugar until light and fluffy. Add eggs; beat until well combined.
3. At low speed, beat in coffee. Then beat in dry ingredients, a third at a time.
4. With spoon, stir in raisins and apricots until well mixed. Refrigerate 1 hour.
5. Meanwhile, preheat oven to 400F. Lightly grease cookie sheets.
6. Drop by rounded teaspoonfuls, 2 inches apart, onto prepared cookie sheets.
7. Bake 8 to 10 minutes, or until hermits are nicely browned. Remove to wire rack; cool.
MAKES ABOUT 8 DOZEN

JUMBO MOLASSES COOKIES

4 cups sifted all-purpose flour
2 teaspoons ground cinnamon
1 teaspoon ground ginger
1 teaspoon baking soda
¼ teaspoon salt
½ cup shortening
1 cup sugar
3 eggs
1 cup light molasses
¼ cup cider vinegar

1. Sift together flour, cinnamon, ginger, baking soda, and salt; set aside.
2. In large bowl of electric mixer, at medium speed, beat shortening, sugar, and eggs until smooth and fluffy.
3. At low speed, beat in molasses and vinegar. Mixture may look curdled. Gradually add flour mixture, beating until smooth.
4. Refrigerate, covered, at least 1 hour.
5. Meanwhile, preheat oven to 375F. Lightly grease cookie sheets.
6. Drop dough by tablespoonfuls*, 3 inches apart, onto prepared cookie sheets. Bake 10 to 12 minutes, or until set. Remove to wire rack; cool.
MAKES ABOUT 3½ DOZEN
*Use a measuring tablespoon.

FUNNY FACES: Before baking, arrange seedless raisins on each cookie, for eyes, nose, and mouth.

LEMON DROPS

2 cups sifted all-purpose flour	2 eggs
1 teaspoon baking powder	2 tablespoons lemon juice
½ teaspoon salt	2 tablespoons grated lemon peel
½ cup butter or regular margarine, softened	Halved candied cherries or pecans (optional)
1 cup sugar	

1. Sift together flour, baking powder, and salt; set aside.
2. In large bowl, with portable electric mixer at medium speed, or wooden spoon, beat butter, sugar, and eggs until smooth and fluffy. Add lemon juice and lemon peel, beating until well combined.
3. Stir in flour mixture, mixing until smooth.
4. Refrigerate dough, covered, at least 1 hour.
5. Preheat oven to 350F. Lightly grease cookie sheets.
6. Drop dough by rounded teaspoonfuls, 2 inches apart, onto prepared cookie sheets. If desired, gently press a cherry or pecan half into center of each.
7. Bake 10 to 12 minutes, or until golden. Remove to wire rack; cool.
MAKES ABOUT 3 DOZEN

PEANUT COOKIES

2 cups sifted all-purpose flour	½ cup maple-flavored syrup
3 teaspoons baking powder	½ cup sugar
2 teaspoons ground cinnamon	2 eggs, beaten
½ teaspoon salt	1 cup salted peanuts, finely chopped
½ cup butter or regular margarine, softened, or shortening	

1. Preheat oven to 350F. Lightly grease cookie sheets.
2. Sift flour with baking powder, cinnamon, and salt; set aside.
3. In large bowl of electric mixer, at medium speed, beat butter, syrup, and sugar until light. Add eggs; beat until well combined.
4. At low speed, add flour mixture, beating just until blended. Stir in peanuts.
5. Drop by rounded teaspoonfuls, 1 inch apart, onto prepared cookie sheets.
6. Bake 12 minutes, or until golden-brown. Remove to wire rack; cool.
MAKES ABOUT 6 DOZEN

PECAN DROPS
(pictured on pages 12-13)

2 cups sifted all-purpose flour	2 tablespoons light cream
¼ teaspoon salt	2 teaspoons vanilla extract
½ cup butter or regular margarine, softened	1 cup coarsely chopped pecans or walnuts
½ cup shortening	
1 cup sifted confectioners' sugar	

1. Preheat oven to 350F.
2. Sift flour with salt; set aside.
3. In large bowl, with wooden spoon, or portable electric mixer at medium speed, beat butter, shortening, sugar, cream, and vanilla until smooth and fluffy.
4. Stir in flour mixture until well combined. Stir in nuts.
5. Drop, by rounded teaspoonfuls, 2 inches apart, onto ungreased cookie sheets. Decorate, if desired, with additional chopped nuts.
6. Bake 15 to 20 minutes, or just until light-golden. Remove to wire rack; cool.
MAKES ABOUT 4 DOZEN

PEANUT-BUTTER DROPS
(pictured on pages 12-13)

1½ cups sifted all-purpose flour	¾ cup chunk-style peanut butter
1 teaspoon baking soda	1 cup light-brown sugar, firmly packed
½ teaspoon salt	2 eggs
1 teaspoon ground ginger	2 tablespoons milk
½ teaspoon ground cloves	1 cup salted Spanish peanuts
¾ cup shortening	

1. Preheat oven to 375F.
2. Sift flour with baking soda, salt, ginger, and cloves; set aside.
3. In large bowl, with wooden spoon, or portable electric mixer at medium speed, beat shortening, peanut butter, and sugar until light and fluffy.
4. Add eggs and milk; beat until smooth. Stir in flour mixture and peanuts until thoroughly combined.
5. Drop by rounded teaspoonfuls, 2 inches apart, onto ungreased cookie sheets. Decorate, if desired, with peanut halves.
6. Bake 10 to 12 minutes, or until golden-brown. Let stand 1 minute. Remove to wire rack; cool.
MAKES ABOUT 3 DOZEN

OATMEAL-NUT COOKIES
(pictured on pages 36-37)

1½ cups sifted all-purpose flour	2 eggs
1 teaspoon baking soda	1 teaspoon vanilla extract
1 teaspoon salt	2 cups uncooked quick-cooking oats
1 cup shortening	1 cup coarsely chopped pecans or walnuts
¾ cup granulated sugar	
¾ cup light-brown sugar, firmly packed	

1. Preheat oven to 375F. Lightly grease cookie sheets.
2. Sift flour with baking soda and salt; set aside.
3. In large bowl, with wooden spoon, or portable electric mixer at medium speed, beat shortening, sugars, eggs, and vanilla until light and fluffy.
4. Stir in flour mixture and oats until well combined. Stir in pecans to make a stiff batter.
5. Drop by slightly rounded teaspoonfuls, 2 inches apart, onto prepared cookie sheets. If desired, decorate with pecan half.
6. Bake 10 to 12 minutes, or until golden-brown. Let stand 1 minute before removing from cookie sheets. Remove to wire rack; cool.
MAKES ABOUT 6 DOZEN

TOASTED OATMEAL COOKIES
(pictured on pages 12-13)

¾ cup butter or regular margarine	½ teaspoon baking soda
2½ cups uncooked rolled oats	1 cup light-brown sugar, firmly packed
½ cup sifted all-purpose flour	1 egg
1 teaspoon ground cinnamon	1 teaspoon vanilla extract
½ teaspoon salt	1 cup coarsely chopped walnuts or pecans (optional)

1. Preheat oven to 375F.
2. In medium skillet, over medium heat, heat butter until lightly browned. Be careful not to burn. Sauté oats, stirring constantly, until golden – about 5 minutes. Remove from heat; cool.
3. Meanwhile, sift flour with cinnamon, salt, and baking soda; set aside.
4. In large bowl, combine sugar, egg, and vanilla. With wooden spoon, or portable electric mixer at medium speed, beat until light and fluffy.
5. Stir in rolled oats and flour mixture until well combined.
6. Drop by slightly rounded teaspoonfuls, 3 inches apart, onto ungreased cookie sheets.
7. Bake 10 to 12 minutes, or until golden. Remove to wire rack; cool.
MAKES ABOUT 4 DOZEN.

GLAZED PINEAPPLE COOKIES
(pictured on pages 36-37)

1 can (8¾ oz) crushed pineapple	1 egg
2 cups sifted all-purpose flour	1 teaspoon vanilla extract
1½ teaspoons baking powder	**Glaze**
¼ teaspoon baking soda	4 cups sifted confectioners' sugar
¼ teaspoon salt	3 to 4 tablespoons liquid from pineapple
½ cup shortening	
1 cup light-brown sugar, firmly packed	

1. Drain pineapple, reserving liquid.
2. Preheat oven to 400F. Lightly grease cookie sheets.
3. Sift flour with baking powder, baking soda, and salt; set aside.
4. In large bowl, with wooden spoon, or portable electric mixer at medium speed, cream shortening with sugar until light.
5. Beat in egg and vanilla until light and fluffy.
6. Add drained pineapple; mix well.
7. Stir in flour mixture until well combined.
8. Drop by rounded teaspoonfuls, 2 inches apart, onto prepared cookie sheets.
9. Bake 8 to 10 minutes, or until golden-brown. Remove to wire rack; cool partially.
10. Meanwhile, make Glaze: In a medium bowl, combine sugar with pineapple liquid; stir until smooth.
11. Spread tops of cookies with glaze while they are still slightly warm.
MAKES ABOUT 3½ DOZEN

RAISIN-SPICE DROPS
(pictured on pages 12-13)

3 cups sifted all-purpose flour	1½ cups light-brown sugar, firmly packed
1 teaspoon baking soda	3 eggs
1 teaspoon salt	1 teaspoon vanilla extract
1 teaspoon ground cinnamon	2 cups seedless raisins
½ teaspoon ground cloves	1 cup coarsely chopped walnuts
1 cup shortening	

1. Sift flour with baking soda, salt, cinnamon, and cloves; set aside.
2. In large bowl of electric mixer, at medium speed, beat shortening, sugar, eggs and vanilla until light and fluffy. At low speed, beat in flour mixture until well combined.
3. Stir in raisins and walnuts. Refrigerate 30 minutes.

4. Meanwhile, preheat oven to 375F. Lightly grease cookie sheets.

5. Drop batter by rounded teaspoonfuls, 2 inches apart, onto prepared cookie sheets. Decorate with more raisins or nuts, if desired.

6. Bake 10 to 12 minutes, or until lightly browned. Remove to wire racks; cool.

MAKES ABOUT 5 DOZEN

GLAZED RAISIN-SPICE DROPS: In medium bowl, combine 3 cups sifted confectioners' sugar with ¼ cup milk and 1 teaspoon vanilla extract; stir until smooth. Use to glaze tops of slightly warm cookies.

SOUR-CREAM CHOCOLATE DROPS

2¾ cups sifted all-purpose flour	2 eggs
½ teaspoon baking soda	1 cup sour cream
½ teaspoon baking powder	1 teaspoon vanilla extract
½ teaspoon salt	1 tablespoon butter or margarine
1 cup corn flakes	3 tablespoons milk
3 squares unsweetened chocolate	1½ cups sifted confectioners' sugar
½ cup soft shortening	
1½ cups granulated sugar	

1. Sift together flour, baking soda, baking powder, and salt. Add corn flakes; set aside.

2. In top of double boiler, over hot water, melt 2 squares chocolate.

3. In large bowl of electric mixer, at medium speed, beat shortening, granulated sugar, and eggs until light and fluffy – about 5 minutes.

4. At low speed, beat in sour cream, vanilla, flour mixture, then chocolate; beat just until combined. Chill dough 1 hour.

5. Preheat oven to 425F. Lightly grease cookie sheets.

6. Drop by rounded teaspoonfuls, 2 inches apart, onto prepared cookie sheets. Bake 8 to 10 minutes. Remove to wire rack; cool.

7. Meanwhile, melt remaining chocolate with butter. Add milk and confectioners' sugar; stir until smooth. Use to frost cooled cookies.

MAKES ABOUT 6 DOZEN

OLD-FASHIONED SOUR CREAM COOKIES

3 cups sifted all-purpose flour	1 cup sour cream
1 teaspoon baking powder	1 teaspoon vanilla, or 2 teaspoons grated lemon peel
½ teaspoon baking soda	
½ teaspoon salt	**Topping**
1 cup butter or regular margarine, softened	½ cup sugar
1½ cups sugar	1 teaspoon ground cinnamon
2 eggs	

1. Sift flour with baking powder, baking soda, and salt; set aside.

2. In large bowl of electric mixer, at medium speed, beat butter, sugar, and eggs until light and fluffy.

3. At low speed, beat in sour cream and vanilla until smooth.

4. Gradually beat in flour mixture until well combined. Refrigerate 1 hour.

5. Meanwhile, preheat oven to 375F. Lightly grease cookie sheets.

6. Drop batter by slightly rounded teaspoonfuls, 2 inches apart, onto prepared cookie sheets.

7. For Topping: Combine ½ cup sugar and cinnamon. Sprinkle a little on unbaked cookies.

8. Bake 10 to 12 minutes, or until golden-brown. Remove to wire rack; cool.

MAKES ABOUT 4 DOZEN

Rolled Cookies

Rolled cookies are made from dough stiff enough to roll thin. Thorough chilling of the dough is one of first principles of successful rolled cookies. If the dough is not well chilled, it will be too soft to roll without adding more flour, and that will make the cookies less tender. The dough should be handled a little at a time, leaving the rest to chill in the refrigerator.

A rolling pin covered with a stockinette, then lightly floured, helps keep the dough from sticking.

Cut cookies close together, to get more cookies from the first rolling. Rerolled cookies are not as tender.

For quick shaping: Roll the dough, and cut with long knife or pastry wheel into squares, diamonds, or rectangles.

For large cookies, like gingerbread men, use a pancake turner or wide metal spatula when placing cookies on cookie sheet.

Start a collection of fancy cookie cutters. Assorted sizes and shapes add interest and variety.

Picture books are full of designs that can be traced onto cardboard and cut out. Place pattern on dough; cut around pattern with sharp point of paring knife. This is a nice way to make cookies for special occasions, such as St. Patrick's Day (shamrock) and New Year's Eve (bell).

Commerically prepared decorating kits are available – you will find tubes and cans with colored icings on the supermarket shelf.

VANILLA COOKIES

1¾ cups sifted all-purpose flour
½ teaspoon baking powder
½ teaspoon salt
½ teaspoon baking soda
½ cup sugar
½ cup butter or regular margarine
1 egg
2 tablespoons milk
1 teaspoon vanilla extract

1. Sift flour with baking powder, salt, baking soda, and sugar into large bowl.
2. With pastry blender or 2 knives, cut butter into flour mixture until consistency of coarse corn meal.
3. With fork, stir in egg, milk, and vanilla; mix well, with hands.
4. Form into a ball. Wrap in waxed paper or foil; refrigerate at least 2 hours.
5. Preheat oven to 350F. Lightly grease cookie sheets. Divide dough into 4 parts.
6. On lightly floured surface, roll each part about ⅛ inch thick. Cut dough into desired shapes.
7. Using spatula, place, 1 inch apart, on prepared cookie sheets. Bake 7 minutes, or until light-golden. Remove to wire racks; cool.
MAKES 5 DOZEN 2-INCH COOKIES

OLD-FASHIONED SUGAR COOKIES

4 cups sifted all-purpose flour
1 teaspoon baking powder
½ teaspoon baking soda
½ teaspoon salt
½ teaspoon ground nutmeg
1 cup butter or regular margarine, softened
1½ cups sugar
1 egg
½ cup sour cream
1 teaspoon vanilla extract

Topping
¼ cup sugar
Raisins or blanched almonds (optional)

1. Sift flour with baking powder, baking soda, salt, and nutmeg; set aside.
2. In large bowl of electric mixer, at medium speed, beat butter, sugar, and egg until light and fluffy.
3. At low speed, beat in sour cream and vanilla until smooth.
4. Gradually add flour mixture, beating until well combined.
5. With rubber scraper, form dough into a ball. Wrap in waxed paper or foil; refrigerate several hours, or overnight.
6. Divide dough into 4 parts. Refrigerate until ready to roll out.
7. Meanwhile, preheat oven to 375F. Lightly grease cookie sheets.
8. On well-floured surface, roll dough, one part at a time ¼ inch thick.
9. With floured, 2½-inch round or scalloped cookie cutter, cut out cookies. Using spatula, place, 2 inches apart, on prepared cookie sheets.
10. Sprinkle tops of cookie with sugar. Place a raisin or almond in the center of each, if desired. Reroll trimmings, and cut.
11. Bake 10 to 12 minutes, or until golden. Remove to wire rack; cool.
MAKES ABOUT 6 DOZEN

LEMON-SUGAR COOKIES

1. Make cookie dough as directed above, omitting nutmeg and vanilla extract.
2. Add 3 tablespoons grated lemon peel and 2 teaspoons lemon extract to dough along with sour cream.
3. For topping, lightly brush unbaked cookies with lemon juice; sprinkle with sugar. (You will need 2 tablespoons lemon juice and 4 tablespoons sugar in all.) Bake as above.

ANNA'S ROLLED COOKIES

3 cups sifted all-purpose flour
1 teaspoon baking powder
1/2 teaspoon salt
3/4 cup butter or regular margarine, softened
1 1/2 cups sugar
2 eggs
1 teaspoon vanilla extract, or 1 tablespoon grated lemon peel

1. Sift flour with baking powder and salt; set aside.
2. In large bowl, with wooden spoon, or portable electric mixer at medium speed, beat butter, sugar, eggs, and vanilla until light and fluffy.
3. Gradually stir in the flour mixture until smooth and well combined.
4. Using rubber scraper, form dough into a ball. Wrap in waxed paper or foil; refrigerate several hours, or overnight.
5. Divide dough into 4 parts; refrigerate until ready to roll out.
6. Preheat oven to 400F. On lightly floured surface, roll dough, one part at a time, about 1/8 inch thick.
7. With floured, 2 1/2-inch round or scalloped cookie cutter, cut out cookies. Using spatula, place 2 inches apart, on ungreased cookie sheets. Reroll trimmings, and cut out.
8. Bake 6 to 8 minutes, or until cookies are set and light-brown around edges. Remove to wire racks; cool.

MAKES 6 DOZEN

LEBKUCHEN ROUNDS

3 cups sifted all-purpose flour
1/2 teaspoon baking soda
1/2 teaspoon salt
1 teaspoon ground allspice
1 teaspoon ground nutmeg
1 teaspoon ground cinnamon
1 teaspoon ground cloves
1 jar (4 oz) citron,* finely chopped
1 can (4 oz) walnuts, finely chopped
1 cup honey
3/4 cup light-brown sugar, firmly packed
1 egg
1 tablespoon lemon juice
2 teaspoons grated lemon peel
2 cups sifted confectioners' sugar
3 tablespoons water

1. Sift flour with baking soda, salt, and spices; set aside. Toss citron with walnuts; set aside.
2. Warm honey in small saucepan. Remove from heat.
3. In large bowl, using portable electric mixer at medium speed, beat brown sugar and egg until smooth and fluffy.
4. Add lemon juice and honey; beat well. Beat in lemon peel and 1 cup flour mixture; beat until smooth.

5. Using wooden spoon, stir in rest of flour mixture until well combined. Then stir in fruit-nut mixture.
6. Refrigerate dough, covered, overnight.
7. Next day, preheat oven to 375F. Lightly grease cookie sheets.
8. On lightly floured surface, roll out dough, one half at a time, 1/4 inch thick. (Refrigerate remaining half until ready to roll out.)
9. Using floured 2-inch round cookie cutter, cut out cookies. Place, 2 inches apart, on prepared cookie sheets. Bake 15 minutes. Remove to wire rack; cool slightly.
10. Meanwhile, make glaze: Combine confectioners' sugar with 3 tablespoons water; stir until smooth.
11. Brush glaze on warm cookies. Decorate with candied-cherry and angelica bits, if desired. Cool completely.
12. Store, tightly covered, 2 to 3 weeks before using. (To make cookies more moist, store with cut piece of apple.)

MAKES 3 DOZEN

*Or use 1/2 cup mixed candied fruit, finely chopped.

MORAVIAN WHITE COOKIES

3 cups sifted all-purpose flour
1 teaspoon baking powder
1/2 teaspoon salt
1 teaspoon ground nutmeg
3/4 cup butter or regular margarine, softened
1 1/4 cups sugar
2 eggs
1 teaspoon vanilla extract

1. Sift flour with baking powder, salt, and nutmeg; set aside.
2. In large bowl, with wooden spoon, or portable electric mixer at medium speed, beat butter, sugar, eggs, and vanilla until smooth and fluffy.
3. With wooden spoon, stir in half of flour mixture. Then add rest of flour mixture, mixing with hands if necessary.
4. Refrigerate dough, covered, several hours, or overnight.
5. Preheat oven to 400F. Divide dough into 4 parts; refrigerate until ready to roll out.
6. On lightly floured surface, roll out dough, one part at a time, 1/8 inch thick.
7. With floured 2 1/2 inch assorted cookie cutters, cut out cookies. Place, 2 inches apart, on ungreased cookie sheets.
8. Bake 8 minutes, or just until set and light-brown around the edges. Remove to wire rack; cool completely. Decorate as desired.

MAKES ABOUT 5 DOZEN

MEXICAN COOKIE KISSES

1 cup sifted all-purpose flour	1 teaspoon ground cinnamon
1/8 teaspoon baking soda	1/2 cup butter or regular margarine, softened
1/8 teaspoon ground nutmeg	1 cup sugar

1. Preheat oven to 400F. Sift flour with baking soda, nutmeg, and cinnamon; set aside.
2. In large bowl of electric mixer, at medium speed, beat butter with sugar until very light and fluffy.
3. At low speed, beat in flour mixture just until well combined.
4. On lightly floured surface, roll dough 1/4 inch thick. Using 2-inch star and heart-shape cookie cutters, cut out dough. Reroll, and cut out leftover dough.
5. Place, 1 1/2 inches apart, on ungreased cookie sheets. Bake 8 to 10 minutes.
6. Remove from oven; let stand on cookie sheets about 2 minutes. Remove to wire rack; cool completely.
MAKES ABOUT 4 DOZEN

GINGERBREAD COOKIES

3 cups sifted all-purpose flour	1/2 cup butter or regular margarine, softened
1/2 teaspoon baking soda	1/2 cup light-brown sugar, firmly packed
1/2 teaspoon salt	1 egg
2 1/2 teaspoons ground ginger	1/2 cup light molasses
1/2 teaspoon ground nutmeg	

1. Sift flour with baking soda, salt, ginger, and nutmeg; set aside.
2. In large bowl of electric mixer, at medium speed, beat butter, sugar, and egg until light and fluffy.
3. At low speed, beat in molasses until smooth. Gradually add flour mixture, beating until smooth and well combined.
4. With rubber scraper, form dough into a ball. Wrap in waxed paper or foil; refrigerate overnight.
5. Divide dough into 4 parts. Refrigerate until ready to roll out.
6. Preheat oven to 375F. Lightly grease cookie sheets.
7. On lightly floured surface, roll dough, one part at a time, 1/4 inch thick. With floured, 2 1/2 inch round cookie cutter, cut out cookies.
8. Using spatula, place, 1 1/2 inches apart, on prepared cookie sheets. Reroll trimmings; cut.
9. Bake 10 to 12 minutes, or until nicely browned. Remove to wire rack; cool.
MAKES 3 DOZEN

SHORTBREAD BALLOONS
(pictured on page 29)

1 cup butter or regular margarine, softened	Decorator Icing, below
1/2 cup sugar	Silver dragées
2 1/2 cups sifted all-purpose flour (sifted before measuring)	Very thin silver cord

1. In large bowl, with portable electric mixer at medium speed, or wooden spoon, beat butter with sugar until light and fluffy.
2. With wooden spoon, stir in flour until smooth and well blended (dough will be stiff).
3. Flatten dough; refrigerate, covered, several hours. Meanwhile, make balloon and gondola designs from cardboard; cover with foil. (See photograph on page 29).
4. Preheat oven to 300F. Divide dough in half; refrigerate until ready to roll out.
5. On lightly floured pastry cloth, using a stockinette-covered rolling pin, roll out each half 1/4 inch thick. Then lay pattern on dough, and cut around it. Press scraps together, and roll out to make a third balloon and gondola.
6. Place balloons and gondolas, 1 inch apart, on ungreased cookie sheets; bake 20 minutes, or until light golden. Remove to wire racks; cool.
7. Make Decorator Icing. Frost as pictured. (See "To Decorate Cookies," page 27.) Pipe frosting through number-3 tip; decorate with dragées, as pictured. Connect balloons to gondolas with silver cord.
MAKES 3 (7-INCH) BALLOONS AND GONDOLAS

CHRISTMAS CUT-OUT COOKIES
(pictured on pages 28-29)

3/4 cup butter or regular margarine, softened	2 cups unsifted all-purpose flour
2/3 cup sugar	
1/4 teaspoon salt	Decorator Icing, page 27
2 egg yolks	Silver dragées
1 tablespoon light cream	
1 teaspoon vanilla extract	

1. Measure butter, sugar and salt into bowl. With electric mixer at medium speed, beat until mixture is smooth.
2. Add egg yolks, cream and vanilla. Beat until fluffy – 2 minutes.
3. Gradually add flour, stirring with wooden spoon until well combined and smooth.
4. With hands or spoon, shape dough into a ball. Place on waxed paper, plastic wrap or foil. Flatten dough and wrap. Refrigerate 2 hours. Dough will be firm.
5. Preheat oven to 325F.
6. On lightly floured pastry cloth, with floured rolling pin, roll out, one fourth at a time, to 1/8 inch thickness. Press together any cracks at edge.
7. With cookie cutters, or using your own patterns as guide, cut out cookies. Place cookies, 1 inch apart, on ungreased cookie sheets.
8. Bake 8 to 10 minutes, or just until edges of cookies are golden.
9. Remove to wire rack; cool completely. Decorate. (See "To Decorate Cookies.")
MAKES 36 ASSORTED LARGE COOKIES

MOLDED COOKIES
(pictured on pages 28-29)

1 cup butter or regular margarine, softened	1/4 cup ground blanched almonds
1 cup sugar	1 egg white
1 teaspoon vanilla extract	2 cups unsifted all-purpose flour
1/4 teaspoon almond extract	Decorator Icing, below Silver dragées

1. In medium bowl, with electric mixer at high speed, beat butter with sugar and vanilla and almond extracts until light and fluffy.
2. Beat in almonds and egg white. With wooden spoon, stir in flour, mixing just until smooth.
3. Refrigerate, covered, 1 hour.
4. Preheat oven to 375F.
5. Press dough into small molds of various shapes- – stars, bows, etc. For shells, we pressed dough into standard-size baking shells. With fingers, press evenly into molds all around.
6. Place molds on cookie sheet. Bake 10 to 12 minutes, or until golden-brown. Larger shells will bake for 15 minutes, or until golden.
7. Remove to wire rack; let cool 3 to 5 minutes in molds. Then carefully loosen around edge, with spatula or sharp knife, and gently turn out of pans. Let cool on wire rack. Decorate. (See "To Decorate Cookies.")
MAKES ABOUT 3 DOZEN ASSORTED COOKIES
Note: If you don't have enough molds, bake a few

at a time. Keep rest of dough refrigerated until ready to use.

DECORATOR ICING

3 egg whites (1/3 cup)	Red, yellow, green and blue food color
3 cups confectioners' sugar	
1/4 teaspoon cream of tartar	

In small bowl of electric mixer, combine egg whites, sugar and cream of tartar. Beat, at high speed, until icing is stiff enough to hold its shape.

TO DECORATE COOKIES

1. Divide icing into several small bowls. Reserve one fourth icing for white icing. Add enough food color to each of remaining bowls to tint desired shades of red, green, blue and yellow. Combine small amounts of color with white to make pink, pale blue, etc. Also, mix some of red and yellow to make orange.
2. Cover each bowl with a damp towel to prevent crust forming on top of icing.
3. Arrange cookies on a flat surface. Frost cookies; use one color frosting at a time on all cookies, if possible. Let dry. Pipe frosting through tube with number-3 tip. Decorate, as pictured, with silver dragées.
4. If cookies are not to be eaten but used for decoration, make cardboard outlines; attach to backs of cookies with rubber cement, to reinforce cookies. Coat them with clear plastic purchased at an art-supply store.
5. Cookies may be arranged against background of Christmas greens, to decorate the table, a mantel, etc. Or they may be hung as ornaments on the Christmas tree.

Stars, Shells, Birds, Butterflies, Balloons—these Fairy-Tale Christmas Cookies are every child's happy dream.

CHOCOLATE COOKIES

2 cups sifted all-purpose flour	1/2 cup butter or regular margarine, softened
1 1/2 teaspoons baking powder	1 cup sugar
1/2 teaspoon baking soda	1 egg
1/4 teaspoon salt	3 envelopes (1-oz size) no-melt unsweetened chocolate
1/2 teaspoon ground cinnamon	

1. Sift flour with baking powder, baking soda, salt, and cinnamon; set aside.
2. In large bowl of electric mixer, at medium speed, cream butter until fluffy. Gradually add sugar, creaming until very light and fluffy.
3. Add egg and chocolate; beat until thoroughly combined.
4. Add flour mixture, a small amount at a time, beating at low speed after each addition.
5. Divide dough in half. Form each half into a ball. Wrap in waxed paper or foil; refrigerate until well chilled – 1 1/2 hours.
6. Cut dough into 8 equal parts. Roll each 1/4 inch thick, between 2 sheets of waxed paper. Refrigerate until thoroughly chilled, for easier handling.
7. Meanwhile, preheat oven to 350F. Lightly grease cookie sheets.
8. Cut dough into desired shapes. Place, 1 inch apart, on prepared cookie sheets. Bake about 8 minutes. Remove to wire racks; cool completely.
MAKES 5 DOZEN 2-INCH COOKIES

GINGER COOKIES

1/3 cup light-brown sugar, firmly packed	2 1/4 teaspoons baking soda
1/3 cup light molasses	1/3 cup butter or regular margarine
3/4 teaspoon ground ginger	1 egg
1/4 teaspoon ground cinnamon	2 1/2 cups sifted all-purpose flour
1/4 teaspoon ground cloves	

1. Combine sugar, molasses, ginger, cinnamon, and cloves in large saucepan; bring to boiling point. Remove from heat.
2. Add baking soda and butter, stirring until mixture thickens and butter melts.

3. Add egg; beat vigorously. Then stir in 2 1/4 cups flour.
4. Put remaining flour on wooden board; place dough on top. Knead until flour is well combined and dough is smooth.
5. Shape into a ball. Wrap in waxed paper or foil; refrigerate 1 1/2 hours until firm.
6. Cut dough into quarters. Roll each about 1/8 inch thick, between 2 sheets of waxed paper. Refrigerate until thoroughly chilled, for easier handling.
7. Meanwhile, preheat oven to 350F. Lightly grease cookie sheets.
8. Cut dough into desired shapes. Using spatula, place, 1 inch apart, on prepared cookie sheets. Bake 5 to 6 minutes. Remove to wire rack; cool.
MAKES 7 DOZEN 2-INCH COOKIES

BETSY McCALL'S
GINGER CUT-OUT COOKIES

2 1/2 cups sifted all-purpose flour	1/2 cup light molasses
1 teaspoon ground ginger	**Frosting**
1/2 teaspoon ground nutmeg	2 cups sifted confectioners' sugar
1/2 teaspoon salt	2 1/2 to 3 tablespoons milk
2 teaspoons baking powder	
1/2 cup shortening	**Decorations**
1/2 cup sugar	Colored sugar
1 egg	Silver dragées
	Multicolored miniature nonpareils

1. Sift together flour, ginger, nutmeg, salt, and baking powder; set aside.
2. In large bowl, with wooden spoon, beat together shortening, sugar, and egg until fluffy (photo a). Add molasses; beat well.
3. Stir in half of flour mixture, mixing until smooth.
4. Add rest of flour mixture, mixing with hands until dough is all one color.
5. With hands, shape dough into a ball; wrap in waxed paper. Refrigerate 2 hours, or overnight.
6. Next day, preheat oven to 375F. Lightly grease cookie sheets.
7. Divide dough into two parts. Return one part to refrigerator.
8. On well-floured board, roll out dough about 1/8 inch thick (photo b).
9. Using assorted cookie cutters, cut out birds, reindeers, etc. (photo c).
10. Slip a pancake turner or spatula under each cookie; lift, and place on prepared cookie sheets, 2 inches apart. (Form leftover dough into a ball; re-roll.) Repeat with remaining dough in refrigerator.

11. Bake 8 to 10 minutes, or until lightly browned (photo d).

12. Remove from pan to wire rack; cool.

13. Make Frosting: In a small bowl, with wooden spoon, beat together confectioners' sugar and milk until smooth. If frosting is too thick, add more milk.

14. Spread frosting over cooled cookies (photo e). Decorate as desired.

MAKES ABOUT 5 DOZEN

GINGERBREAD MEN

1. Make and roll out dough as directed above.

2. Using 5-inch gingerbread-man cutter, cut out cookies.

3. Bake and frost as directed above.

4. To decorate: Mark eyes, nose, and buttons with raisins; mouth with cinnamon candies.

MAKES 20

CHRISTMAS TREES

1. Make and roll out dough as directed above.

2. Using 6½-inch Christmas-tree cutter, cut out cookies.

3. Bake and frost as directed above. Decorate as desired.

MAKES 15

SWISS CINNAMON CRISPS

3 cups sifted all-purpose
 flour
½ teaspoon salt
1 tablespoon ground
 cinnamon
1 cup butter or regular
 margarine, softened
½ cup light-brown sugar,
 firmly packed

¾ cup granulated sugar
1 egg

Topping
2 tablespoons milk
1 egg
½ cup granulated sugar
1 tablespoon ground
 cinnamon

1. Sift flour with salt and cinnamon; set aside.
2. In large bowl, with wooden spoon, or portable electric mixer at medium speed, beat butter, sugars, and egg until light and fluffy.
3. Gradually add flour mixture, stirring until smooth and well combined.
4. With rubber scraper, form dough into a ball. Wrap in waxed paper or foil; refrigerate 1 hour.
5. Divide dough into 4 parts. Refrigerate until ready to roll out.
6. Meanwhile, preheat oven to 375F. Make Topping: In small bowl, with rotary beater, combine milk and egg. In another small bowl, combine sugar and cinnamon; set aside.
7. On lightly floured surface, roll dough, one part at a time, into a 9-by-7-inch rectangle. With floured sharp knife or pastry wheel, cut into 16 rectangles.
8. Using spatula, place, 1½ inches apart, on ungreased cookie sheets. Brush top of cookies lightly with egg mixture; then sprinkle with sugar mixture.
9. Bake 10 to 12 minutes, or until set and golden-brown. Remove to wire rack; cool.
MAKES 64

ENGLISH RAISIN COOKIES

3½ cups sifted all-
 purpose flour
½ teaspoon baking soda
½ teaspoon salt
1 teaspoon ground
 cinnamon
1 teaspoon ground
 nutmeg

½ cup butter or regular
 margarine, softened
1 cup sugar
2 eggs
½ cup sour cream
1 cup finely chopped
 raisins or walnuts

1. Sift flour with baking soda, salt, cinnamon, and nutmeg; set aside.
2. In large bowl, with wooden spoon or portable electric mixer at medium speed, beat butter, sugar, and eggs until light and fluffy.

3. Add sour cream, raisins, and flour mixture; mix thoroughly.
4. With rubber scraper, form dough into a ball. Wrap in waxed paper or foil; refrigerate 1 hour.
5. Divide dough into four parts; refrigerate until ready to roll out.
6. Meanwhile, preheat oven to 375F. Lightly grease cookie sheets.
7. On lightly floured surface, roll dough, one part at a time, into a 12-by-14-inch rectangle. With sharp, floured knife, cut dough on the diagonal to make diamond shapes, or cut into 18 bars.
8. Using spatula, place, 1½ inches apart, on prepared cookie sheets. Reroll trimmings, and cut.
9. Bake 8 to 10 minutes, or until golden-brown. Remove to wire racks; cool.
MAKES 6 DOZEN

ORANGE-COCOA SUGAR COOKIES

Cookie Dough
3½ cups sifted all-
 purpose flour
½ cup sifted
 unsweetened cocoa
1 teaspoon baking
 powder
½ teaspoon baking soda
½ teaspoon salt
¼ teaspoon ground
 nutmeg

1 cup butter or regular
 margarine, softened
1½ cups sugar
1 egg
½ cup sour cream
2 tablespoons grated
 orange peel

¼ cup sifted
 unsweetened cocoa
¼ cup sugar

1. Make Cookie Dough: Sift flour with ½ cup cocoa, baking powder, soda, salt, nutmeg; set aside.
2. In large bowl of electric mixer, at medium speed, beat butter, 1½ cups sugar, and egg until light and fluffy.
3. At low speed, beat in sour cream and orange peel until smooth.
4. Gradually add flour mixture, beating until well combined.
5. With rubber scraper, form dough into a ball. Wrap in waxed paper or foil; refrigerate several hours, or overnight.
6. Divide dough into 4 parts. Refrigerate until ready to roll out.
7. Meanwhile, preheat oven to 375F. Lightly grease cookie sheets.

8. Combine ¼ cup cocoa and ¼ cup sugar; sprinkle some on wooden board or pastry cloth; roll dough over, one part at a time, in mixture, coating completely. (Sprinkle board with rest of cocoa-sugar mixture as necessary.)

9. Roll out dough ¼ inch thick. With floured, 2½-inch, round or scalloped cookie cutter, cut out cookies. Using spatula, place, 2 inches apart, on prepared cookie sheets.

10. Bake 10 to 12 minutes or until cookies are set. Remove to wire rack; cool.

MAKES 4 DOZEN

WALNUT-TOPPED COOKIES
(pictured on pages 36-37)

3 cups sifted all-purpose flour	1 egg
½ teaspoon salt	**Topping**
1 cup butter or regular margarine, softened	2 tablespoons milk
	1 egg
½ cup light-brown sugar, firmly packed	½ cup coarsely chopped walnuts or pecans
¾ cup granulated sugar	¼ cup granulated sugar

1. Sift flour with salt; set aside.

2. In large bowl, with wooden spoon, or portable electric mixer at medium speed, beat butter, sugars, and egg until light and fluffy.

3. Stir in flour mixture until smooth and well combined.

4. Form dough into a ball. Wrap in waxed paper or foil; refrigerate 1 hour.

5. Divide dough into 4 parts. Refrigerate until ready to roll out.

6. Meanwhile, preheat oven to 375F. Make Topping: In small bowl, with rotary beater, beat milk and egg together. In another small bowl, combine walnuts and sugar. Set aside.

7. On lightly floured surface, roll dough, one part at a time, about ⅛ inch thick.

8. With floured 2½ inch round or scalloped cookie cutter, cut out cookies. Using spatula, place, 1½ inches apart, on ungreased cookie sheets. Reroll trimmings, and cut.

9. Lightly brush tops of cookies with egg mixture; then sprinkle with nut mixture.

10. Bake 10 to 12 minutes, or until golden. Remove to wire racks; cool.

MAKES ABOUT 8 DOZEN

WALNUT SHORTBREAD COOKIES: Proceed as directed above, rolling dough ¼ inch thick instead of ⅛ inch. Makes about 4 dozen.

LEMON HEARTS

1½ cups ground pecans or hazelnuts	2 tablespoons lemon juice
⅓ cup sifted all-purpose flour	**Glaze**
½ teaspoon baking powder	1 cup sifted confectioners' sugar
2 tablespoons grated lemon peel	1½ tablespoons lemon juice
3 egg yolks	Few drops yellow food color (optional)
⅔ cup granulated sugar	

1. In small bowl, lightly toss pecans with flour, baking powder, and lemon peel; set aside.

2. In small bowl of electric mixer, at high speed, beat egg yolks until thick and lemon-colored. Gradually add ⅔ cup sugar, beating until mixture is smooth and well blended – about 5 minutes.

3. At low speed, add lemon juice, beating just until combined.

4. With wooden spoon, stir in nut mixture; mix to combine well.

5. Refrigerate, covered, overnight.

6. Next day, preheat oven to 325F. Generously grease and flour cookie sheets.

7. On lightly sugared surface, roll out dough ¼ inch thick.

8. With 2-inch heart-shaped cookie cutter, cut out cookies.

9. Place, 1 inch apart, on prepared cookie sheets. Bake 12 to 15 minutes, or just until cookies are puffed and set.

10. Meanwhile, make Glaze: In small bowl, combine confectioners' sugar, lemon juice, and food color; stir until smooth.

11. Remove cookies to wire rack; cool partially. Spread tops of warm cookies with glaze. Decorate, if desired, with cinnamon candies; cool completely.

MAKES ABOUT 4½ DOZEN

MORE ABOUT NUTS

To blanch nuts: Cover shelled nuts with cold water; bring to boil. Remove from heat; drain. Press each nut between fingers, so husk will slip off easily; then drain dry on paper towels.

To sliver: Blanch nuts as above. Then with sharp knife, slice moist nuts lengthwise into long, thin slivers.

To grind nuts Put shelled nuts through fine blade of food chopper, or use small hand grinder, electric blender or food processor. (Be careful not to grind nuts too fine.)

To store: Keep shelled nuts in tightly covered container in refrigerator. Store unshelled nuts in bag in the refrigerator.

OLD-FASHIONED FILLED COOKIES

3 cups sifted all-purpose
  flour
1 teaspoon baking
  powder
½ teaspoon salt
¾ cup butter or regular
  margarine, softened
1½ cups sugar
2 eggs
1 teaspoon vanilla
  extract, or 1
  tablespoon grated
  lemon peel

Filling
1 pkg (8 oz) pitted dates,
  cut up; or 1 cup
  seedless raisins
½ cup sugar
1 teaspoon grated lemon
  peel
¼ cup lemon juice
½ cup coarsely chopped
  walnuts

1. Sift flour with baking powder and salt; set aside.
2. In large bowl, with wooden spoon, or portable electric mixer at medium speed, beat butter, sugar, eggs, and vanilla until light and fluffy.
3. Gradually stir in the flour mixture until smooth and well combined.
4. Using rubber scraper, form dough into a ball. Wrap in waxed paper or foil; refrigerate several hours, or overnight.
5. Divide dough into 4 parts; refrigerate until ready to use.
6. Meanwhile, make Filling: In small saucepan, combine dates and sugar with ½ cup water. Cook, stirring and over medium heat, until mixture has thickened – about 5 minutes. Remove from heat. Stir in lemon peel, lemon juice, and walnuts. Cool completely.
7. Preheat oven to 375F. Lightly grease cookie sheets.
8. On lightly floured surface, roll dough, one part at a time, ⅛ inch thick. With floured, 2½-inch round or scalloped cookie cutter, cut out cookies. Reroll trimmings, and cut.
9. Using spatula, place half the cookies, 2 inches apart, on prepared cookie sheets. Spread 1 teaspoon filling over each cookie; cover with another cookie. With floured fork, seal edges firmly; also prick center of top.
10. Bake 10 to 12 minutes, or until lightly browned. Remove to wire rack; cool.
MAKES 3 DOZEN

FILLED TURNOVERS

1. Prepare cookie dough and filling as above.
2. On lightly floured surface, roll dough, one part at a time, into a 10-by-12-inch rectangle. With floured, sharp knife, cut into 12 rectangles.
3. Using spatula, place, 2 inches apart, on prepared cookie sheets. Spread 1 teaspoon filling on half of each; fold over. With floured fork, seal edges firmly; prick center of tops.
4. Bake as above. Remove to wire rack; cool.
MAKES 4 DOZEN

ALMOND-RASPBERRY COOKIES
(pictured on pages 36-37)

1½ cups sifted all-
  purpose flour
1 tablespoon
  unsweetened cocoa
1 teaspoon ground
  cinnamon
¾ cup sugar
½ cup ground
  unblanched almonds

1 tablespoon grated
  lemon peel
½ cup butter or regular
  margarine
1 egg, slightly beaten
½ cup raspberry jam
1 egg yolk
2 tablespoons water

1. Sift flour, cocoa, cinnamon, and sugar into medium bowl; stir in almonds and lemon peel.
2. Add butter; cut in with pastry blender or 2 knives until mixture is like coarse cornmeal.
3. Stir in egg, mixing with hands until dough holds together.
4. Refrigerate, covered, 1 hour.
5. Preheat oven to 375F.
6. On lightly floured surface, roll half of dough ⅛ inch thick. With floured 2-inch oval or scalloped cookie cutter, cut out cookies.
7. Using spatula, place, 1 inch apart, on ungreased cookie sheets. Spread each cookie with ½ teaspoon raspberry jam, ¼ inch from edge.
8. Roll out remaining half of dough; cut out cookies. With 1-inch cutter, cut out centers to make rings. Reroll centers; bake as desired.
9. Place rings on top of jam-covered cookies.
10. Brush tops lightly with egg yolk beaten with 2 tablespoons water.
11. Bake 10 to 12 minutes, or until golden-brown. Remove to wire rack; cool completely.
MAKES ABOUT 3 DOZEN

GROSSMUTTER'S FILLED COOKIES

4 cups sifted all-purpose
  flour
3 teaspoons baking
  powder
¼ teaspoon salt
1 cup butter or regular
  margarine, softened
1 cup sugar
1 egg
½ cup milk
1 teaspoon vanilla
  extract

Filling
1¼ cups dark raisins,
  chopped
8 pitted dates, chopped
½ cup sugar
1 teaspoon all-purpose
  flour
¾ cup water

1. Sift flour with baking powder and salt; set aside.
2. In large bowl, with wooden spoon, beat butter,

sugar, and egg until mixture is smooth and light. Stir in milk and vanilla.

3. Add flour mixture; stir until well combined. Refrigerate, covered, at least 4 hours, or overnight.

4. Make Filling: In small saucepan, combine filling ingredients with ¾ cup water; mix well.

5. Cook, stirring and over medium heat, until thickened – 10 to 15 minutes. Refrigerate until ready to use.

6. Preheat oven to 350F. On lightly floured surface, roll half of dough ⅛ inch thick.

7. Cut into rounds with lightly floured 2-inch cookie cutter; place rounds, 1½ inches apart, on ungreased cookie sheets.

8. Place 1 teaspoon filling in center of each round.

9. Roll other half of dough ⅛ inch thick; cut into rounds. Top each filled round with a plain round. Press edges together firmly with tines of fork.

10. Bake 15 to 18 minutes, or until golden- brown.

MAKES ABOUT 3½ DOZEN

SWEDISH WAFERS

1 cup butter or regular margarine, softened	2 cups sifted all-purpose flour
⅓ cup heavy cream	Granulated sugar
1 teaspoon vanilla extract	⅓ cup strawberry or raspberry jam

1. In medium bowl, with wooden spoon, or portable electric mixer at medium speed, beat butter, cream, vanilla, and flour until smooth and thoroughly combined.

2. Using rubber scraper, form dough into a ball. Wrap in waxed paper or foil; refrigerate at least 1 hour.

3. Divide dough into 4 parts; refrigerate each until ready to roll out.

4. Meanwhile, preheat oven to 375F. On well-floured surface, roll dough, one part at a time, ⅛ inch thick. Sprinkle surface of dough lightly with granulated sugar.

5. With floured, 1½-inch round cookie cutter, cut out cookies. Using spatula, place, 1 inch apart, on ungreased cookie sheets. Reroll trimmings, and cut. Prick surface of each cookie 3 times with fork.

6. Bake until puffy and delicately browned – about 8 or 9 minutes. Remove to wire rack; cool.

7. Just before serving, put 2 cookies together, sandwich-fashion, with about ¼ teaspoon jam.

MAKES 5 DOZEN COOKIE SANDWICHES

VIENNA TARTS

½ cup butter or regular margarine, softened	1 egg yolk
1 pkg (3 oz) cream cheese, softened	2 tablespoons milk
1 cup sifted all-purpose flour	¼ cup finely chopped nuts
About 3 tablespoons red currant, raspberry, strawberry or grape jelly	Confectioners' sugar

1. With wooden spoon, cream butter and cheese until light. Stir in flour, mixing well. Refrigerate 1 hour.

2. Meanwhile, preheat oven to 400F.

3. Turn out dough onto lightly floured surface; roll out into 12-inch square. With sharp knife or pastry wheel, cut into 2-inch squares.

4. Place about ¼ teaspoon jelly near center of each square. Fold over to form a triangle; press edges to seal.

5. Brush top of each with mixture of egg yolk beaten with milk; sprinkle with nuts.

6. Place on ungreased cookie sheets; bake 8 to 10 minutes, or until golden. Sprinkle with confectioners' sugar; let cool on wire rack.

MAKES 3 DOZEN

Glazed Pineapple Cookies

Peanut-Butter Pinwheels

Ground-Raisin Cookies

Brazil-Nut Cookies

Oatmeal-Nut Cookies

Almond-Raspberry Cookies

MOLDED COOKIES have the some-
what symmetrical form of rolled cookies. The stiff cookie doughs
are shaped, sometimes with the palms of the hands, into small
balls. Some are forced through a cookie press into many and
fancy shapes. Most of the doughs should be refrigerated
at least an hour, so they can be handled more easily.

Walnut-Topped Cookies

Jewel Cookies

CHEWY CHOCOLATE BALLS

1 can (8 oz) walnuts
3 squares unsweetened
  chocolate, cut up
¼ cup unsifted all-
  purpose flour
¼ cup packaged dry
  bread crumbs

¼ teaspoon ground
  cloves
2 eggs
1 cup granulated sugar
Confectioners' sugar

1. In electric blender, grind walnuts, then chocolate, until fine.
2. In large bowl, combine walnuts, chocolate, flour, bread crumbs, and cloves; set aside.
3. In small bowl of electric mixer at high speed, beat eggs until light.
4. Gradually add granulated sugar, 1 tablespoon at a time, beating until smooth and fluffy – about 5 minutes.
5. Add to walnut mixture; stir until well combined. Refrigerate several hours or overnight.
6. Meanwhile, preheat oven to 375F. Lightly grease cookie sheets.
7. Using hands, roll dough into balls, 1 inch in diameter. Roll in confectioners' sugar. Place, 2 inches apart, on prepared cookie sheets.
8. Bake 10 to 12 minutes, or until surfaces of cookies appear cracked.
9. Cool on wire rack; roll again in confectioners' sugar.
MAKES ABOUT 4 DOZEN

CHOCOLATE-PRINT COOKIES

½ cup butter or regular
  margarine, softened
¼ cup light-brown sugar
  firmly packed
1 egg yolk
1 teaspoon vanilla
  extract
1 cup sifted all-purpose
  flour
1 egg white, slightly
  beaten

¾ cup flaked coconut

Chocolate Filling
½ cup semisweet-
  chocolate pieces
2 tablespoons water
2½ tablespoons cream
  cheese, softened
½ teaspoon vanilla
  extract
⅛ teaspoon salt

1. In medium bowl, with portable electric mixer at medium speed, or wooden spoon, beat butter with sugar until light and fluffy. Beat in egg yolk and vanilla.
2. At low speed, gradually beat in flour; continue beating until smooth.
3. Refrigerate dough, covered, about 1 hour, or until it is stiff enough to handle.

4. Preheat oven to 350F. Using hands, roll dough into balls 1¼ inches in diameter.
5. Dip balls into egg white; then roll in coconut. Place, 1½ inches apart, on ungreased cookie sheets.
6. With finger, make a depression in center of each cookie. Bake 15 minutes, or until light- golden. Let cool on wire rack.
7. Make Chocolate Filling: Melt chocolate with 2 tablespoons water over hot, not boiling, water.
8. Remove from heat. Gradually stir in cheese, vanilla, and salt, mixing until smooth.
9. Use chocolate mixture to fill depressions in center of cookies.
MAKES ABOUT 2 DOZEN

OLD-FASHIONED JUMBLES

3 cups sifted all-purpose
  flour
½ teaspoon salt
1 tablespoon ground
  cinnamon
1 cup butter or regular
  margarine, softened

1 cup sugar
2 eggs
1 teaspoon vanilla
  extract
Salad oil
Granulated sugar

1. Sift flour with salt and cinnamon; set aside.
2. In large bowl, with wooden spoon, or portable electric mixer at medium speed, beat butter, 1 cup sugar, eggs, and vanilla until creamy and smooth.
3. Gradually add flour mixture, stirring until well blended. Refrigerate 1 hour.
4. Meanwhile, preheat oven to 375F. Lightly grease cookie sheets.
5. Using hands, roll dough into balls 1¼ inches in diameter. Place, 2 inches apart, on prepared cookie sheets. Flatten with bottom of glass brushed with salad oil, then dipped in sugar. (Redip bottom of glass in sugar frequently.)
6. Bake 10 to 12 minutes, or until light-brown. Remove to wire rack; cool.
MAKES ABOUT 5 DOZEN

COFFEE-ALMOND LACE WAFERS

½ cup ground blanched
  almonds
½ cup butter or regular
  margarine, softened
½ cup sugar

2 teaspoons instant
  coffee
1 tablespoon all-purpose
  flour
2 tablespoons milk

1. Preheat oven to 375F. Generously grease and flour well 2 cookie sheets.
2. Combine all ingredients in small saucepan; cook, stirring, over low heat, until butter is melted.

3. Drop by teaspoonfuls, 4 inches apart, onto prepared cookie sheets, placing 4 or 5 on each cookie sheet.

4. Bake, one cookie sheet at a time, about 6 minutes, or until wafers are just lightly browned and bubbly.

5. Let stand on cookie sheet about 1 minute. Loosen each with spatula. Then, working quickly, roll each wafer around handle of wooden spoon. Let cool, seam side down, on wire rack.

6. Grease and flour cookie sheet before each baking. If cookies cool too much before rolling, reheat a minute or two in oven.

7. Let cookies stand, uncovered, at room temperature until serving.

MAKES ABOUT 2½ DOZEN

CRISSCROSS PEANUT COOKIES

1¼ cups sifted all-purpose flour	½ cup light-brown sugar, firmly packed
¾ teaspoon baking soda	½ cup granulated sugar
½ cup butter or regular margarine, softened	1 egg
½ cup chunk-style peanut butter	1 teaspoon vanilla extract

1. Sift flour with baking soda; set aside.

2. In large bowl, with portable electric mixer at medium speed, or wooden spoon, combine butter with remaining ingredients; beat until smooth and fluffy.

3. With wooden spoon, stir in flour mixture until well combined.

4. Refrigerate, covered, at least 1 hour.

5. Preheat oven to 375F. Lightly grease cookie sheets.

6. Form dough into 1¼-inch balls. Place, 3 inches apart, on prepared cookie sheets.

7. Flatten with fork, dipped in flour, making a crisscross pattern. Bake 10 to 12 minutes, or until lightly browned.

8. Remove to wire rack; cool.

MAKES ABOUT 5 DOZEN

RICH CHOCOLATE COOKIE SANDWICHES

2 cups sifted all-purpose flour	**Filling**
2 teaspoons baking powder	3 cups sifted confectioners' sugar
¾ cup butter or regular margarine, softened	2 tablespoons butter or regular margarine, softened
¾ cup granulated sugar	2 tablespoons light cream
1 teaspoon vanilla	1 teaspoon vanilla
2 envelopes (1-oz size) no-melt unsweetened chocolate	

1. Sift together flour, and baking powder; set aside.

2. In large bowl, with portable electric mixer at medium speed, beat butter, sugar, and vanilla until smooth and fluffy. Add chocolate, beating until combined.

3. Stir in flour mixture, blending well.

4. Refrigerate dough, covered, at least 1 hour.

5. Preheat oven to 350F. Lightly grease cookie sheets.

6. Form dough into balls 1 inch in diameter. Place, 3 inches apart, on prepared cookie sheets.

7. With palm of hand, flatten each cookie to a circle ⅛ inch thick.

8. Bake 10 to 12 minutes, or just until set but not browned. Cool 5 minutes before removing to wire rack; let cool completely.

9. Meanwhile, make Filling: In small bowl, combine sugar, butter, cream, and vanilla; beat with portable electric mixer at medium speed until smooth.

10. Just before serving, put 2 cookies together, sandwich fashion, with 1 tablespoon filling.

MAKES ABOUT 27 COOKIE SANDWICHES

COCONUT COOKIES

1¾ cups sifted all-purpose flour	2 eggs
½ teaspoon baking powder	1 teaspoon vanilla extract
¼ teaspoon salt	1 can (3½ oz) flaked coconut
½ cup butter or regular margarine, softened	½ cup finely chopped almonds
1½ cups sugar	

1. Sift flour with baking powder and salt; set aside.

2. In large bowl, with wooden spoon, or portable electric mixer at medium speed, beat butter and sugar until light and fluffy. Beat in eggs and vanilla until smooth.

3. Add flour mixture; stir just until combined. Refrigerate 1 hour.

4. Meanwhile, preheat oven to 400F. Lightly grease cookie sheets. Combine coconut and almonds on sheet of waxed paper.

5. Drop dough by slightly rounded teaspoonfuls onto coconut mixture; roll to coat completely. Using hands, roll dough into balls. Place, 2 inches apart, on prepared cookie sheets.

6. Bake 12 to 15 minutes, or until golden. (Cookies will flatten during baking.) Remove to wire rack; cool.

MAKES ABOUT 5 DOZEN

GINGER-SUGAR COOKIES

2 cups sifted all-purpose flour	1 teaspoon ground ginger
2 teaspoons baking soda	1/4 teaspoon salt
1 teaspoon ground cinnamon	1 1/3 cups sugar
1 teaspoon ground cloves	3/4 cup soft shortening
	1/4 cup light molasses
	1 egg

1. Preheat oven to 375F. Lightly grease cookie sheets.
2. Sift flour with baking soda, cinnamon, cloves, ginger, and salt; set aside.
3. In large bowl of electric mixer, at medium speed, gradually add 1 cup sugar to shortening, creaming until very light and fluffy – about 5 minutes. Blend in molasses and egg.
4. At low speed, beat in flour mixture just until well mixed, scraping down side of bowl with rubber scraper. Refrigerate 1 hour.
5. Pinch off pieces of dough; shape into 1 1/4 inch balls. Roll in remaining sugar.
6. Place, 2 1/2 inches apart, on prepared cookie sheets; bake 8 to 10 minutes, or until golden-brown. Remove to wire rack; cool. These cookies will have a crinkled surface.
MAKES 3 1/2 DOZEN

GINGER CRINKLES

2 1/4 cups sifted all-purpose flour	3/4 cup soft shortening
2 teaspoons baking soda	1 cup light-brown sugar, firmly packed
1/4 teaspoon salt	1 egg
1 teaspoon ground cinnamon	1/4 cup light molasses
1 teaspoon ground ginger	Granulated sugar
1/2 teaspoon ground cloves	Water

1. Sift flour with baking soda, salt, and spices; set aside.
2. In large bowl of electric mixer, at medium speed, beat shortening, brown sugar, and egg until light and fluffy.
3. Beat in molasses until smooth.
4. At low speed, beat in flour mixture just until well combined. Refrigerate at least 1 hour.

5. Meanwhile, preheat oven to 375F. Lightly grease cookie sheets.
6. With hands, roll slightly rounded teaspoonfuls of dough into balls 1 1/4 inches in diameter. Dip tops in granulated sugar. Place, sugar side up, 3 inches apart, on prepared cookie sheets.
7. Sprinkle each cookie with 2 or 3 drops of water.
8. Bake 10 to 12 minutes, or until golden. Remove to wire racks; cool.
MAKES 3 1/2 DOZEN

GROUND-RAISIN COOKIES
(pictured on pages 36-37)

3 cups sifted all-purpose flour	1 cup sugar
1/2 teaspoon baking soda	2 eggs
1/2 teaspoon salt	1/4 cup sour cream
1 teaspoon ground cinnamon	1 cup ground or finely chopped raisins
1 teaspoon ground nutmeg	Salad oil
3/4 cup butter or regular margarine, softened	Granulated sugar

1. Sift flour with baking soda, salt, cinnamon, and nutmeg; set aside.
2. In large bowl, with portable electric mixer at medium speed, beat butter, 1 cup sugar, and eggs until light and fluffy.
3. Add sour cream, raisins, and flour mixture; mix thoroughly.
4. With rubber scraper, form dough into a ball. Wrap in waxed paper or foil; refrigerate 1 hour.
5. Meanwhile, preheat oven to 375F. Lightly grease cookie sheets.
6. Using hands, form dough into balls 1 inch in diameter.
7. Place, 2 inches apart, on prepared cookie sheets. Flatten with bottom of glass brushed with salad oil, then dipped in sugar. (Redip bottom of glass in sugar frequently.)
8. Bake 10 to 12 minutes, or until golden-brown. Remove to wire racks: cool.
MAKES ABOUT 5 DOZEN

JEWEL COOKIES
(pictured on pages 36-37)

1/2 cup butter or regular margarine, softened	1 egg white, slightly beaten
1/4 cup light-brown sugar, firmly packed	1 cup finely chopped walnuts or pecans
1 egg yolk	2 tablespoons currant jelly
1 teaspoon vanilla extract	
1 cup sifted all-purpose flour	

1. In medium bowl, with wooden spoon, beat butter, sugar, egg yolk, and vanilla until smooth.
2. Stir in flour just until combined. Refrigerate 30 minutes.
3. Meanwhile, preheat oven to 375F. Using hands, roll dough into balls 1 inch in diameter. Dip in egg white; then roll in walnuts.
4. Place 1 inch apart, on ungreased cookie sheets. With thimble or thumb, press center of each cookie.
5. Bake 10 to 12 minutes, or until a delicate golden-brown. Remove to wire rack; cool.
6. Place ¼ teaspoon jelly in center of each cookie. (Diced candied fruit may be used, instead of jelly, if desired.)
MAKES 2 DOZEN

KRIS KRINGLES
(pictured on page 42)

½ cup butter or regular margarine, softened
½ cup sugar
3 hard-cooked egg yolks, sieved
1 raw egg yolk
½ teaspoon ground cardamom
1 tablespoon grated lemon peel

2 cups sifted all-purpose flour
1 egg white
1 tablespoon water

Topping
½ cup finely sliced almonds
2 tablespoons sugar

1. Preheat oven to 375F. Lightly grease cookie sheets.
2. In medium bowl, with wooden spoon, beat butter, sugar, hard-cooked and raw egg yolks, cardamom and lemon peel until well combined.
3. Stir in flour; mix with hands to blend thoroughly. Dough will be stiff.
4. Divide dough into two parts. On lightly floured surface, roll out each part into a 7-by-6-inch rectangle.
5. Cut each rectangle in half lengthwise; then cut crosswise into 12 strips. You will have 48 strips.
6. With palms of hand, roll each strip to make it 4 inches long. Form each into a ring; pinch ends together, to seal.

7. Place on prepared cookie sheets, 1 inch apart. Brush with egg white beaten with 1 tablespoon water.
8. **Make topping:** Combine almonds with sugar. Sprinkle over tops of cookies.
9. Bake cookies 10 to 12 minutes, or until golden-brown. Remove to wire rack, cool.
MAKES 4 DOZEN

VIENNESE CRESCENTS

Cookie Dough
2 cups sifted all-purpose flour
1 cup butter or regular margarine, softened
1 cup ground unblanched almonds or hazelnuts
½ cup sifted confectioners' sugar

1 teaspoon vanilla extract
¼ teaspoon almond extract

Vanilla Sugar
3-inch piece vanilla bean, cut up
2 cups sifted confectioners' sugar

1. **Make Cookie Dough:** In large bowl, combine all ingredients. With hands, mix until thoroughly blended. Refrigerate, covered, 1 hour.
2. **Make Vanilla Sugar:** In electric blender, combine cut-up vanilla bean and ¼ cup confectioners' sugar. Cover; blend at high speed about 8 seconds. Combine with remaining confectioners' sugar on a large sheet of foil.
3. Preheat oven to 375F.
4. Shape cookies: Form dough into 1-inch balls; then, with palms of hands, roll each ball into a roll 3 inches long.
5. Place, 2 inches apart, on ungreased cookie sheets; curve each to make crescent.
6. Bake 12 to 15 minutes, or until set but not brown.
7. Let stand 1 minute before removing. With spatula, place hot cookies in vanilla sugar; turn gently to coat both sides. Cool completely.
8. Just before serving, coat with additional vanilla sugar, if desired.
MAKES ABOUT 4 DOZEN

TUDOR ROSES

½ cup butter or regular margarine, softened
½ cup unsifted confectioners' sugar
¾ cup sifted all-purpose flour
¼ teaspoon ground mace
½ teaspoon vanilla extract

1. Preheat oven to 350F.
2. In small bowl of electric mixer, at medium speed, cream butter until light and fluffy. Gradually beat in sugar.
3. Sift together flour and mace; beat into butter mixture, along with vanilla.
4. Onto ungreased cookie sheet, press dough through cookie press or pastry bag, using star tip. Place cookies 1 inch apart.
5. Bake 15 minutes, or until a delicate golden-brown. Cool on cookie sheet several minutes. Remove to wire rack; cool.
MAKES ABOUT 3 DOZEN

CINNAMON TEACAKES

1 cup butter or regular margarine, softened
1½ cups confectioners' sugar
2¼ cups sifted all-purpose flour
1 teaspoon ground cinnamon
¼ teaspoon salt
1 teaspoon vanilla extract

1. In large bowl of electric mixer, at medium speed, beat butter until light and fluffy.
2. Then, at low speed, blend in ½ cup sugar, the flour, ½ teaspoon cinnamon, the salt, and vanilla extract (dough will be rather stiff). Chill in refrigerator 30 minutes, or until stiff enough to handle easily.
3. Preheat oven to 400F. Lightly grease cookie sheets.
4. With fingers roll dough into 1-inch balls.
5. Place balls, 2 inches apart, on prepared cookie sheets; bake 9 to 10 minutes, or until a delicate golden-brown.
6. On piece of waxed paper, combine remaining sugar and cinnamon. Roll hot teacakes in this mixture. Place on wire racks; cool.
MAKES ABOUT 3½ DOZEN

The elegant white American porcelain jar is filled with the heavenly Hazelnut Balls also shown with Kris Kringles on the dish; a tiny white porcelain Italian villa is really a box, crammed to the roof with both delicious kinds. (Recipes on pages 41 and 58.)

Bar Cookies

Bar cookies have a rich, cake-like texture. Easy to make, they store and ship well. They are made in a large pan, cooled and then cut into bars or squares. Best known, and best loved, of the bar cookies are brownies; we've added some that are less known but equally good. Bar cookies, with a dish of applesauce, stewed rhubarb, or fruit compote, make an ideal dessert, especially for children.

When baking in ovenproof glass pans, reduce oven temperature by 25F.

Store bar cookies right in the baking pan, tightly covered with foil or plastic wrap.

A ruler is handy to mark off even squares or bars.

APRICOT SHORTBREAD
(pictured on pages 44-45)

Shortbread	Filling
⅓ cup soft butter or regular margarine	¾ cup dried apricots
½ cup light-brown sugar, firmly packed	Water
	1 teaspoon grated lemon peel
1 cup sifted all-purpose flour	⅔ cup granulated sugar
	2 teaspoons cornstarch
	⅓ cup chopped walnuts

1. Preheat oven to 350F.
2. Make Shortbread: In medium bowl, with portable electric mixer, beat butter with sugar until light and fluffy.
3. At low speed, beat in flour.
4. Pat mixture evenly into bottom of an 8-by-8-by-2-inch baking pan. Bake 12 minutes, or until light-golden in color. Let cool completely in pan on wire rack.
5. Meanwhile, make Filling: Place apricots in small saucepan. Add just enough water to cover; bring to boiling. Reduce heat, and simmer, covered, 15 minutes. Drain apricots, reserving 3 tablespoons cooking liquid.
6. Chop apricots fine. Combine in small saucepan with reserved liquid, lemon peel, sugar, cornstarch. Bring to boiling, stirring; boil 1 minute.
7. Let filling cool 10 minutes. Spread evenly over shortbread crust. Sprinkle with walnuts.
8. Bake 20 minutes. Let cool completely in pan on wire rack. Cut into bars.
MAKES 20

Apricot Shortbread
Chocolate-Chip-Butterscotch Bars
Frosted Chocolate-Almond Brownies
Oatmeal-Fudge Bars
California Raisin Bars

APPLESAUCE-SPICE SQUARES

2 cups sifted all-purpose flour
2 teaspoons baking soda
3/4 teaspoon ground cinnamon
1/4 teaspoon ground cloves
1/4 teaspoon ground nutmeg
1/2 cup butter or regular margarine, softened
1 cup granulated sugar
1 egg
1 teaspoon vanilla extract
1 1/2 cups canned applesauce
1 cup coarsely chopped walnuts or pecans
1 cup raisins
Confectioners' sugar

1. Preheat oven to 350F. Lightly grease a 15 1/2-by-10 1/2-by-1-inch jelly-roll pan.
2. Sift flour with baking soda, cinnamon, cloves, and nutmeg; set aside.
3. In large bowl of electric mixer, at medium speed, cream butter with granulated sugar until light and fluffy.
4. Add egg and vanilla; beat well, scraping down side of bowl with rubber scraper.
5. At low speed, beat in flour mixture just until combined.
6. Add applesauce, walnuts, and raisins; stir with spoon, until well mixed.
7. Turn into prepared pan; bake about 25 minutes, or just until surface springs back when gently pressed with fingertip. Cool on wire rack. Sprinkle with confectioners' sugar. Cut into squares.
MAKES 35

TUTTI-FRUTTI SQUARES

3/4 cup unsifted all-purpose flour
1 teaspoon baking powder
1/2 teaspoon salt
1/4 cup butter or regular margarine, softened
3/4 cup granulated sugar
2 eggs
1 cup chopped walnuts or pecans
1 cup chopped dates
3/4 cup mixed candied fruit

Glaze
1 1/2 cups sifted confectioners' sugar
2 tablespoons milk

1. Preheat oven to 325F. Sift together flour, baking powder and salt; set aside. Lightly grease bottom of a 15 1/2-by-10 1/2-by-1-inch jelly-roll pan; line pan with waxed paper, and grease lightly.
2. In large bowl, with electric mixer at medium speed, or wooden spoon, beat butter, granulated sugar and eggs until smooth and fluffy.
3. Stir in nuts, dates and candied fruit; mix well.
4. Stir in the sifted dry ingredients. Spread mixture in prepared pan.
5. Bake 35 minutes, or until golden-brown. Remove to wire rack; cool. Remove from pan, and peel off waxed paper.
6. Make glaze: In small bowl, combine confectioners' sugar and milk. Drizzle lengthwise and then across. Cut into 48 squares.
MAKES 48

BUTTERSCOTCH-PEANUT BARS

½ cup butter or regular margarine, softened
1½ cups light-brown sugar, firmly packed
½ cup chunk-style peanut butter
1¼ cups sifted all-purpose flour

1 teaspoon baking powder
½ teaspoon salt
2 eggs
1 teaspoon vanilla extract

1. Melt butter in 2-quart saucepan. Add brown sugar and peanut butter; mix well.
2. Bring just to boiling, over low heat, stirring constantly. Remove from heat; let cool to lukewarm.
3. Sift flour with baking powder and salt. Set aside.
4. Meanwhile, preheat oven to 300F. Lightly grease a 13-by-9-by-2-inch baking pan.
5. With wooden spoon, beat eggs and vanilla into cooled peanut-butter mixture. Stir in flour mixture.
6. Spread mixture evenly in prepared pan. Bake 45 minutes, or until lightly browned.
7. Let cool in pan on wire rack. While slightly warm, cut into bars.
MAKES 32

DATE-NUT BARS

½ cup sifted all-purpose flour
1 teaspoon baking powder
¼ teaspoon salt
2 eggs

1 cup granulated sugar
1 pkg (8 oz) pitted dates, finely chopped
1 cup coarsely chopped walnuts
Confectioners' sugar

1. Preheat oven to 350F. Lightly grease a 13-by-9-by-2-inch pan.
2. Sift flour with baking powder and salt; set aside.
3. In small bowl of electric mixer, at medium speed, beat eggs until light.
4. Gradually add granulated sugar, beating until smooth and fluffy.
5. At low speed, beat in flour mixture until well combined.
6. Stir in dates and nuts; mix thoroughly. Spread evenly in prepared pan.
7. Bake 25 to 30 minutes, or until golden. Cool slightly.
8. With sharp knife, cut into bars while still warm. Let cool completely in pan before removing. To serve, roll in confectioners' sugar.
MAKES 30

FROSTED CHOCOLATE-ALMOND BROWNIES
(pictured on pages 44-45)

2 squares unsweetened chocolate
¾ cup sifted all-purpose flour
½ teaspoon baking powder
½ teaspoon salt
½ cup soft shortening

1 cup granulated sugar
2 eggs, unbeaten
½ teaspoon almond extract
½ cup chopped almonds
Chocolate Frosting, page 47
Blanched almonds

1. Preheat oven to 350F. Lightly grease an 8-by-8-by-2-inch baking pan. Then melt the unsweetened chocolate, in top of a double boiler, over hot, not boiling, water.
2. Sift flour with baking powder and salt. In medium bowl, using a wooden spoon, beat the shortening with the sugar until light. Beat in eggs, one at a time, then the almond extract and the melted chocolate.
3. Stir in flour mixture and chopped almonds. Turn into prepared pan. Bake 25 to 30 minutes, or until the surface is firm to the touch. Cool right in the pan on wire rack.
4. Frost; top with blanched almonds.
MAKES 15

CHOCOLATE-CHIP BUTTERSCOTCH BARS
(pictured on pages 44-45)

¾ cup sifted all-purpose flour
½ teaspoon baking powder
½ teaspoon salt
½ cup butter or regular margarine, softened
1 cup dark-brown sugar, firmly packed
2 eggs

1 teaspoon vanilla extract
1 pkg (6 oz) semisweet-chocolate pieces
½ cup chopped nuts
Butterscotch Frosting, page 47
½ cup semisweet-chocolate pieces

1. Preheat oven to 350F. Grease an 8-by-8-by-2-inch baking dish.
2. Sift flour with baking powder and salt. Set aside.
3. Melt butter in small saucepan. Add sugar; stir, over low heat, until sugar is melted.
4. Turn into medium bowl; add eggs, one at a time, beating well after each addition. Add vanilla.
5. Stir in flour mixture, 1 package chocolate, and the nuts, mixing well.
6. Turn into prepared pan. Bake 30 minutes.
7. Let cool completely in pan on wire rack. Frost with Butterscotch Frosting; garnish with chocolate pieces. Cut into bars.
MAKES 20

CHOCOLATE FROSTING

1 square unsweetened
  chocolate
2 tablespoons butter or
  regular margarine,
  softened
2 tablespoons light
  cream

1 cup sifted
  confectioners' sugar
1/2 teaspoon vanilla
  extract

1. Melt chocolate over hot, not boiling, water; let cool.
2. In small bowl, combine butter, cream, and sugar; beat until smooth.
3. Stir in cooled chocolate and the vanilla, blending well. Use to frost tops of Chocolate-Almond Brownies, page 46.
MAKES 3/4 CUP

BUTTERSCOTCH FROSTING

1/3 cup butter or regular
  margarine, softened
1/2 cup light-brown sugar,
  firmly packed

1 tablespoon light cream
1/4 teaspoon vanilla
  extract

1. In medium bowl, with portable electric mixer at high speed, beat butter until light. Gradually beat in sugar; beat until fluffy.
2. At low speed, beat in cream and vanilla. Use to spread over Chocolate-Chip Butterscotch Bars, page 46. (If frosting seems too soft to spread, refrigerate 10 minutes before using.)
MAKES 1 CUP

QUICK BUTTERSCOTCH BROWNIES

1/2 cup sifted all-purpose
  flour
1/4 cup sugar
1/2 teaspoon baking
  powder
1/4 teaspoon salt
2 eggs
2 pkg (3⅝-oz size)
  butterscotch-pudding
  and pie-filling mix

1/3 cup butter or regular
  margarine, softened
1/2 teaspoon vanilla
  extract
1/2 cup chopped walnuts
1/2 cup semisweet-
  chocolate pieces

1. Preheat oven to 325F. Lightly grease a 9-by-9-by-1¾-inch pan.
2. Sift flour with sugar, baking powder, and salt; set aside.
3. In large bowl, with rotary beater, beat eggs until very thick. Add flour mixture and rest of ingredients; stir to mix well.
4. Turn into prepared pan; bake 35 to 40 minutes, or until cake tester inserted in center comes out clean.

5. Let cool slightly in pan, placed on wire rack. Cut into bars.
MAKES 2 DOZEN

MARBLED BROWNIES

1 cup sifted all-purpose
  flour
1/4 teaspoon baking
  powder
1/4 teaspoon salt
1/2 cup butter or regular
  margarine, softened
1½ cups sugar

2 eggs
1 teaspoon vanilla
  extract
1 cup coarsely chopped
  walnuts or pecans
2 envelopes (1-oz size)
  no-melt unsweetened
  chocolate

1. Preheat oven to 350F. Lightly grease a 9-by-9-by-1¾-inch pan.
2. Sift flour with baking powder and salt; set aside.
3. In large bowl, with portable electric mixer, at medium speed, beat butter, sugar, eggs, and vanilla until light.
4. Stir in flour mixture and nuts until well combined.
5. Divide batter in half. Stir chocolate into one half, mixing well.
6. Spoon plain and chocolate batters, alternately, into prepared pan. To marble: With spatula or knife, cut through batter to form a "Z."
7. Bake 25 to 30 minutes. Cool 10 minutes.
8. With sharp knife, cut into squares. Cool completely in pan.
MAKES 16

PEANUT BROWNIES

2 squares unsweetened
  chocolate
1/2 cup shortening
1 cup sugar
2 eggs
1/2 teaspoon vanilla
  extract

1/2 cup sifted all-purpose
  flour
1/4 teaspoon baking
  powder
3/4 cup coarsely chopped
  salted peanuts

1. Preheat oven to 350F. Lightly grease a 9-by-9-by-1¾-inch pan.
2. In top of double boiler, melt chocolate and shortening over hot, not boiling, water. Remove from hot water.
3. With wooden spoon, beat in sugar, eggs, and vanilla, mixing well.
4. Sift flour with baking powder into chocolate mixture; stir to mix well. Stir in peanuts.
5. Turn mixture into prepared pan; bake 30 minutes.
6. Let cool in pan on wire rack. Cut into squares.
MAKES 16

CHOCOLATE BROWNIES

2 squares unsweetened chocolate	¼ teaspoon salt
½ cup butter or regular margarine, softened	1 cup sugar
	2 eggs
¾ cup sifted all-purpose flour	1 teaspoon vanilla extract
½ teaspoon baking powder	1 cup coarsely chopped walnuts or pecans

1. Preheat oven to 350F. Lightly grease an 8-by-8-by-2-inch pan.
2. Melt chocolate with butter over hot, not boiling, water. Cool.
3. Sift flour with baking powder and salt; set aside.
4. In a large bowl, with wooden spoon, or portable electric mixer at medium speed, beat sugar and eggs until light.
5. Beat in chocolate mixture and vanilla.
6. Stir in flour mixture and nuts until well combined.
7. Spread evenly in prepared pan. Bake 25 to 30 minutes, or just until surface is firm to the touch.
8. Cool 10 minutes. With sharp knife, cut into 16 squares.
MAKES 16

ROCKY-ROAD BROWNIES: Spread batter in lightly greased 13-by-9-by-2-inch pan. Bake 20 minutes. Cover immediately with 1 package (6¼ oz) miniature marshmallows. Let stand. Meanwhile, melt 1 package (6 oz) semisweet- chocolate pieces over hot, not boiling, water. Spoon over marshmallows, spreading to cover. Cool completely in pan. Refrigerate just until chocolate is set – about 1 hour. Cut into bars.
MAKES 30

BROWN-SUGAR BROWNIES

1⅓ cups sifted all-purpose flour	1 cup light-brown sugar, firmly packed
1 teaspoon baking powder	1 egg
½ teaspoon salt	1 teaspoon vanilla extract
½ cup butter or regular margarine, softened	½ cup coarsely chopped walnuts

1. Preheat oven to 350F. Lightly grease a 9-by-9-by-1¾-inch pan.
2. Sift flour with baking powder and salt; set aside.
3. In large bowl, with wooden spoon, or portable electric mixer at medium speed, beat butter, sugar, egg, and vanilla until smooth.
4. Stir in flour mixture and nuts until well blended. Spread evenly in prepared pan.

5. Bake 25 to 30 minutes, or until surface springs back when gently pressed with fingertip. Cool slightly.
6. With sharp knife, cut into bars while still warm.
MAKES 20

CHOCOLATE BROWN-SUGAR BROWNIES: Stir 1 package (6 oz) semisweet-chocolate pieces into batter along with nuts. Bake in lightly greased 13-by-9-by-2-inch pan 30 minutes. Cool slightly. Cut into bars while still warm.
MAKES 2 DOZEN

COCONUT LEMON BARS

Cookie Crust	Filling
½ cup butter or regular margarine, softened	4 eggs
	2 cups granulated sugar
½ cup confectioners' sugar, sifted	⅓ cup lemon juice
	¼ cup all-purpose flour
2 cups sifted all-purpose flour	1½ teaspoons baking powder
	1 can (3½ oz) flaked coconut

1. Preheat oven to 350F.
2. Make cookie crust: In medium bowl, cream butter and confectioners' sugar with wooden spoon until smooth.
3. With hands, work in 2 cups flour until mixture is smooth.
4. Pat into bottom of a 13-by-9-by-2-inch pan; bake 20 minutes, or until golden. Cool on wire rack.
5. Meanwhile, make filling: In small bowl, using electric mixer, beat eggs until light. Gradually beat in granulated sugar. Add lemon juice, flour, sifted with baking powder, beating just until combined. Stir in coconut.
6. Pour evenly over cooled crust; bake 25 minutes, or until firm to the touch.
7. Cool 20 minutes. With sharp knife, cut into 30 bars while still warm. If desired, sprinkle with confectioners' sugar.
MAKES 30 BARS

CHINESE CHEWS

¾ cup sifted all-purpose flour	¾ cup sugar
½ teaspoon baking powder	1 pkg (8 oz) pitted dates, chopped
¼ teaspoon salt	½ cup chopped nuts
2 eggs	1 teaspoon grated lemon peel

1. Preheat oven to 325F. Lightly grease a 9-by-9-by-1¾-inch baking pan.

2. Sift flour with baking powder and salt.

3. In medium bowl, with rotary beater or portable electric mixer, beat eggs with sugar until thick and light.

4. Stir in flour mixture, dates, nuts, and lemon peel until well combined.

5. Turn into prepared pan. Bake 30 minutes, or until lightly browned and top is firm.

6. Let cool completely in pan. Cut into bars.
MAKES 2 DOZEN

COCONUT-CHOCOLATE-CHIP SQUARES

3½ cups sifted all-purpose flour

1 teaspoon baking soda

½ teaspoon salt

½ teaspoon ground cinnamon

¼ teaspoon ground nutmeg

⅔ cup butter or regular margarine

2 teaspoons vanilla extract

1 teaspoon almond extract

1 cup light-brown sugar, firmly packed

1 cup granulated sugar

1 egg

1½ cups semisweet chocolate pieces

½ cup flaked coconut

½ cup yogurt or sour cream

1. Line a 15½-by-10½-by-1-inch jelly-roll pan with waxed paper. Sift together flour, baking soda, salt, cinnamon, and nutmeg; set aside.

2. In large bowl of electric mixer, at low speed, cream butter with extracts until fluffy. Gradually beat in sugars. Add egg; mix well.

3. Stir in chocolate and coconut.

4. Stir in flour mixture alternately with yogurt, beginning and ending with flour mixture.

5. Spread in prepared pan; refrigerate overnight.

6. Next day, preheat oven to 400F.

7. Invert pan; remove mixture, and peel off paper. Cut with sharp knife, into 48 squares, each 1¾ by 1¾ inches.

8. Place, 2 inches apart, on ungreased cookie sheet. Bake 13 minutes, or until deep golden-brown.
MAKES 4 DOZEN

CHOCOLATE-BUTTERSCOTCH PICNIC BARS

2 cups sifted all-purpose flour

1 teaspoon baking soda

1 teaspoon salt

2 teaspoons ground cinnamon

¾ cup butter, regular margarine, or shortening

1 cup sugar

2 eggs

½ cup chopped walnuts

1 pkg (6 oz) semisweet chocolate pieces

1 pkg (6 oz) butterscotch pieces

1. Preheat oven to 350F. Lightly grease an 11½-by-7½-by-2-inch disposable foil pan, or 13-by-9-by-2-inch pan.

2. Sift flour with baking soda, salt, and cinnamon; set aside.

3. In large bowl of electric mixer, at medium speed, cream butter with sugar until light and fluffy. Beat in eggs.

4. At low speed, beat in flour mixture just until combined. Stir in nuts. Divide dough in half. Stir chocolate into one half and butterscotch into other.

5. Spread chocolate mixture in half of prepared pan and butterscotch mixture in other half; bake 30 minutes.

6. Let cool, in pan, on wire rack. Cut into bars.
MAKES 64

CRISPY CHOCOLATE STICKS

Cookie Layer

1 square unsweetened chocolate

¼ cup butter or regular margarine

1 egg

½ cup granulated sugar

¾ cup sifted all-purpose flour

¼ cup chopped pecans

Filling

2 tablespoons butter or regular margarine, softened

1 cup sifted confectioners' sugar

1 tablespoon heavy cream or evaporated milk

¼ teaspoon vanilla extract

Glaze

1 square unsweetened chocolate

1 tablespoon butter or margarine

1. Preheat oven to 350F. Grease an 8-by-8-by-2-inch pan.

2. Make Cookie Layer: Melt chocolate and butter together over hot water. Cool slightly.

3. In medium bowl, beat egg until frothy. Stir in chocolate mixture and sugar. Add flour and pecans, stirring until well blended.

4. Turn into prepared pan; bake 20 minutes. Cool thoroughly on wire rack.

5. Make Filling: In small bowl, blend all ingredients. Spread over cookie layer. Chill at least 10 minutes.

6. Make Glaze: Melt chocolate and butter together over hot water. Pour over filling, tilting pan so glaze will flow evenly. Refrigerate 15 minutes, to harden glaze.

7. With sharp knife, cut into sticks.
MAKES 18

DUTCH NUT STRIPS

1 cup sifted all-purpose flour	1 teaspoon vanilla extract
1/8 teaspoon salt	1/2 cup finely chopped walnuts or pecans
1/2 cup butter or regular margarine, softened	
1/2 cup light-brown sugar, firmly packed	

1. Preheat oven to 375F. Sift flour with salt; set aside.
2. In large bowl, using wooden spoon, beat butter, brown sugar, and vanilla until smooth and fluffy.
3. Add flour mixture, mixing until well combined. Stir in nuts.
4. With palms of hands, pat dough evenly onto an ungreased cookie sheet to form a rectangle 10 inches wide and 15 inches long.
5. Bake 10 to 12 minutes, or until golden-brown.
6. Immediately cut hot cookies, with sharp knife, into strips 1 inch wide and 2½ inches long.
7. Remove to wire rack; cool completely.

MAKES 5 DOZEN

DREAM BARS

Cookie Crust

1/2 cup butter or regular margarine, softened	1 teaspoon vanilla extract
1/2 cup light-brown sugar, firmly packed	3 tablespoons all-purpose flour
1 cup sifted all-purpose flour	1/4 teaspoon salt
	1 teaspoon baking powder

Filling

2 eggs	1 can (3½ oz) flaked coconut
1 cup light-brown sugar, firmly packed	1 cup coarsely chopped walnuts or pecans

1. Preheat oven to 350F.
2. Make Cookie Crust: In small bowl, cream butter and sugar, with wooden spoon, until smooth.
3. With hands, work in flour until mixture is smooth.
4. Pat into bottom of a 13-by-9-by-2-inch ungreased pan. Bake 10 minutes, or until golden. Cool on wire rack.
5. Meanwhile, make Filling: In small bowl of electric mixer, at medium speed, beat eggs until light.
6. Gradually beat in sugar. Add vanilla, flour, salt, and baking powder, beating just until combined.
7. Stir in coconut and walnuts.
8. Spread evenly over cooled crust. Bake 25 minutes, or until golden and firm to the touch. Cool slightly.
9. With sharp knife, cut into bars.

MAKES 30

OATMEAL-FUDGE BARS
(pictured on pages 44-45)

Oatmeal Layer	**Fudge Layer**
1/2 cup soft shortening	1 pkg (6 oz) semisweet-chocolate pieces
1 cup light-brown sugar, firmly packed	1 tablespoon butter or regular margarine, softened
1 egg	1/3 cup sweetened condensed milk
1/2 teaspoon vanilla extract	1/4 teaspoon salt
3/4 cup sifted all-purpose flour	1/2 cup chopped walnuts
1/2 teaspoon baking soda	1 teaspoon vanilla extract
1/2 teaspoon salt	
2 cups uncooked quick-cooking oats	
1/2 cup chopped walnuts	

1. Make Oatmeal Layer: Grease a 9-by-9-by-1¾-inch baking pan.
2. In medium bowl, with wooden spoon, beat shortening with sugar until fluffy. Beat in egg and vanilla.
3. Sift flour with baking soda and salt into sugar mixture; mix well. Stir in oats and nuts.
4. Remove 1 cup mixture for topping. Press rest of mixture into bottom of prepared pan.
5. Make Fudge Layer: Preheat oven to 350F.
6. In small saucepan, combine chocolate pieces, butter, milk, and salt.
7. Cook, stirring, over low heat until chocolate and butter are melted.
8. Remove from heat; stir in nuts and vanilla.
9. Spread chocolate mixture over oatmeal layer. Sprinkle top with reserved oat mixture.
10. Bake 25 minutes, or until surface is lightly browned.
11. Let cool completely in pan on wire rack. Cut into bars.

MAKES 2 DOZEN

APRICOT-OATMEAL BARS

1 cup dried apricots	1 cup light-brown sugar, firmly packed

Cookie Crust

1/2 cup butter or regular margarine, softened	1 teaspoon vanilla extract
1/2 cup light-brown sugar, firmly packed	1/4 teaspoon baking powder
2 cups uncooked quick-cooking oats	1/2 cup roasted diced almonds
	1 cup uncooked quick-cooking oats

Filling

2 eggs	1 tablespoon all-purpose flour

1. In small saucepan, combine apricots with just enough water to cover. Cook, covered, 30 minutes, or until tender. Drain apricots well. Chop finely; set aside.

2. Preheat oven to 350F. Lightly grease an 8-by-8-by-2-inch pan.

3. Make Cookie Crust: In large bowl, using portable electric mixer or wooden spoon, beat butter with sugar until light and fluffy. With rubber scraper, fold oats into sugar mixture.

4. Using hands, spread mixture evenly over bottom of prepared pan. Bake 15 minutes. Let cool.

5. Make Filling: In large bowl of electric mixer, at high speed, beat eggs until light. Beat in sugar, vanilla, and baking powder.

6. With rubber scraper, fold in apricots, almonds, 1 cup oats, and the flour, combining well. Turn onto cooled crust.

7. Bake 30 to 35 minutes, or until the top is golden and firm to the touch.

8. Let cool completely in pan on wire rack.

9. Then cut into 2½-by-1-inch bars.

MAKES 2 DOZEN

SCOTCH OATMEAL SHORTBREAD

3 cups uncooked quick-cooking oats	½ teaspoon salt
⅔ cup sugar	¾ cup butter or regular margarine, softened
½ cup sifted all-purpose flour	1 teaspoon vanilla extract

1. Preheat oven to 350F. Lightly grease a 13-by-9-by-2-inch pan.

2. In large bowl, combine oats, sugar, flour, and salt.

3. With pastry blender or 2 knives, cut in butter until mixture resembles coarse cornmeal. Stir in vanilla; mix well.

4. With hands, press mixture evenly into prepared pan.

5. Bake 25 to 30 minutes, or until golden. Cool slightly.

6. Cut into bars while still warm. Let cool completely in pan before removing.

MAKES 32

FILLED OATMEAL-DATE BARS

Date Filling	Oatmeal Crust
2 pkg (8-oz size) pitted dates, cut up	1½ cups sifted all-purpose flour
½ cup granulated sugar	½ teaspoon baking soda
1 cup water	½ teaspoon salt
¼ cup lemon juice	¾ cup butter or regular margarine, softened
½ cup coarsely chopped walnuts	1 cup light-brown sugar, firmly packed
	1½ cups uncooked quick-cooking oats

1. Make Date Filling: In small saucepan, combine dates and sugar with 1 cup water. Over medium heat, cook, stirring constantly, until mixture is thickened – about 5 minutes. Remove from heat. Stir in lemon juice and nuts; cool.

2. Meanwhile, preheat oven to 375F. Lightly grease a 13-by-9-by-2-inch pan.

3. Make Oatmeal Crust: Sift flour with baking soda and salt; set aside.

4. In medium bowl, with wooden spoon, or portable electric mixer at medium speed, beat butter and sugar until light and fluffy. Add flour mixture and oats. With hands, mix until well combined.

5. Press half oatmeal mixture, evenly, into bottom of prepared pan. Spread with filling. Cover with remaining oatmeal mixture; press lightly with hands.

6. Bake 25 to 30 minutes, or until golden. Cool slightly.

7. Cut into bars while still warm.

MAKES 32

FILLED OATMEAL-MINCEMEAT BARS: In small bowl, combine 2 cups prepared mincemeat, ½ cup coarsely chopped walnuts, and 1 tablespoon grated orange peel. Use instead of Date Filling.

HONEY-FRUIT BARS

2¼ cups sifted all-purpose flour	1 teaspoon vanilla extract
½ teaspoon baking soda	½ cup honey
¼ teaspoon salt	1 cup seedless raisins
½ cup butter or regular margarine, softened	1 jar (4 oz) diced candied orange or mixed peel
½ cup light-brown sugar, firmly packed	1 cup finely chopped walnuts
2 eggs	Confectioners' sugar

1. Preheat oven to 350F. Lightly grease a 13-by-9-by-2-inch pan. Sift flour with baking soda and salt; set aside.

2. In large bowl, with wooden spoon, or portable electric mixer at medium speed, beat butter, brown sugar, eggs, vanilla and honey until smooth and fluffy.

3. With wooden spoon, stir in flour mixture until well combined. Then stir in raisins, peel, and nuts, mixing well.

4. Spread evenly in prepared pan. Bake 25 to 30 minutes, or until cake tester inserted in center comes out clean.

5. Remove to wire rack; cool partially. With sharp knife, cut into bars while still warm. Let cool completely in pan before removing. To serve, sprinkle with confectioners' sugar.

MAKES 3 DOZEN

PINEAPPLE-GRAHAM BARS

¼ cup butter or regular margarine, softened
½ cup light-brown sugar, firmly packed
1 egg
½ cup sifted all-purpose flour

½ cup graham-cracker crumbs
1 can (8½ oz) crushed pineapple, drained
½ cup chopped walnuts

1. Preheat oven to 350F. Lightly grease an 8-by-8-by-2-inch baking pan.
2. In medium bowl, with wooden spoon or portable electric mixer, beat butter with sugar until light and fluffy. Beat in egg.
3. Stir in flour, crumbs, pineapple, and walnuts. Turn into prepared pan.
4. Bake 30 to 35 minutes, or until browned and surface is firm.
5. Let cool completely in pan. Cut into bars.
MAKES 20

PINEAPPLE BARS

Cookie Crust
½ cup butter or regular margarine, softened
¼ cup granulated sugar
1 cup sifted all-purpose flour

Filling
⅓ cup sifted all-purpose flour
½ teaspoon baking powder

¼ teaspoon salt
2 eggs
1 cup light-brown sugar, firmly packed
½ teaspoon almond extract
½ cup coarsely chopped walnuts
1 cup drained canned crushed pineapple

Confectioners' sugar

1. Preheat oven to 350F. Lightly grease a 9-by-9-by-1¾-inch pan.
2. Make Cookie Crust: In small bowl, cream butter and sugar with wooden spoon until creamy. With hands, work in flour until mixture is smooth.
3. Pat into bottom of prepared pan. Bake 25 minutes, or only until golden. Cool on wire rack.
4. Meanwhile, make Filling: Sift flour with baking powder and salt; set aside.
5. In small bowl of electric mixer, at medium speed, beat eggs slightly. Gradually beat in brown sugar.

6. With spoon, blend in flour mixture just until combined. Fold in almond extract, walnuts, and pineapple.
7. Spread evenly over cooled crust. Bake 30 minutes, or until browned and firm to the touch. Cool on wire rack.
8. Cut into bars. Sprinkle lightly with confectioners' sugar.
MAKES 2 DOZEN

DELICIOUS PRUNE BARS

Cookie Crust
½ cup butter or regular margarine, softened
½ cup light-brown sugar, firmly packed
1 cup sifted all-purpose flour

Prune Filling
1¼ cups dried prunes (about 20)
Water
⅓ cup light-brown sugar, firmly packed

2 tablespoons cornstarch
⅛ teaspoon salt
1 tablespoon grated orange peel
¼ cup orange juice
1 cup coarsely chopped walnuts
2 eggs
1 can (3½ oz) flaked coconut

1. Preheat oven to 350F.
2. Make Cookie Crust: In small bowl of electric mixer, at medium speed, cream butter with sugar until light and fluffy.
3. At low speed, beat in flour. Mixture will be creamy.
4. Pat dough evenly into bottom of a 9-by-9-by-1¾-inch ungreased pan. Bake 10 to 12 minutes, or until light-golden. Let cool at least 15 minutes.
5. Meanwhile, make Prune Filling: In medium saucepan, over medium heat, cook prunes in just enough water to cover, 30 minutes. Drain, reserving 2 tablespoons liquid.
6. Remove pits; with scissors, cut prunes into quarters.
7. Combine prunes in saucepan with reserved liquid, sugar, cornstarch, salt, orange peel and juice; bring to boil. Reduce heat; simmer, stirring constantly, 2 to 3 minutes, or until thickened. Stir in walnuts. Spread over crust.

8. In small bowl, beat eggs just until frothy. Stir in coconut.
9. Spread evenly over prune mixture. Bake 25 minutes. Cool slightly.
10. With sharp knife, cut into bars.
MAKES 2 DOZEN

PINEAPPLE-COCONUT SQUARES

½ cup butter or regular margarine, softened	1 egg, well beaten
¾ cup sugar	1 tablespoon butter or margarine, melted
1¼ cups sifted all-purpose flour	½ teaspoon vanilla extract
1 can (1 lb, 4 oz) crushed pineapple, well drained	1 can (3½ oz) flaked coconut

1. Preheat oven to 350F.
2. In small bowl of electric mixer, at medium speed, cream butter with ¼ cup sugar until light and fluffy. Gradually beat in flour, to form a soft dough.
3. Press dough evenly on bottom and ½ inch up sides of 9-by-9-by-1¾-inch ungreased pan.
4. Bake 15 minutes, or until golden-brown. Let cool.
5. Spread pineapple evenly over crust.
6. Add rest of sugar to egg; beat just until blended. Add melted butter, vanilla, coconut.
7. Spread mixture over pineapple; bake 20 minutes, or until top is golden-brown.
8. When cool, cut into 1½-inch squares.
MAKES 3 DOZEN

CALIFORNIA RAISIN BARS
(pictured on pages 44-45)

1 medium orange, halved	2½ cups sifted all-purpose flour
1 cup dark raisins	3 teaspoons baking powder
⅓ cup chopped walnuts	1 teaspoon salt
⅔ cup butter or regular margarine, softened	2 eggs, beaten
1½ cups light-brown sugar, firmly packed	½ cup milk

1. Preheat oven to 375F. Squeeze juice from orange. Set juice aside.

2. Cut up orange. Put through coarse blade of food chopper with raisins and walnuts.
3. In large bowl, combine butter with sugar, mixing well. Stir in flour to make a crumbly mixture.
4. Remove 2 cups flour mixture; press into bottom of 13-by-9-by-2-inch baking pan.
5. Stir baking powder and salt into rest of flour mixture.
6. Combine eggs, milk, and orange juice; stir. Pour into flour mixture along with raisin mixture; mix well.
7. Pour over cookie layer in baking pan. Bake 30 to 35 minutes, or until golden-brown.
8. Let cool completely in pan on wire rack. Cut into bars.
MAKES 32

TOFFEE BARS

Cookie Crust	½ cup uncooked quick-cooking oats
½ cup butter or regular margarine, softened	
½ cup light-brown sugar, firmly packed	**Topping**
1 egg yolk	3 squares semisweet chocolate
1 teaspoon vanilla extract	1 tablespoon butter or margarine
½ cup sifted all-purpose flour	½ cup coarsely chopped walnuts or pecans

1. Preheat oven to 375F. Lightly grease a 13-by-9-by-2-inch pan.
2. Make Cookie Crust: In large bowl, with wooden spoon, or portable electric mixer at medium speed, beat butter, sugar, egg yolk, and vanilla until smooth.
3. Add flour and oats; stir to combine well.
4. Press mixture evenly in bottom of prepared pan.
5. Bake 15 minutes, or until golden. Cool slightly.
6. Meanwhile, make Topping: Melt chocolate and butter over hot, not boiling, water.
7. Spread over warm cookie crust; sprinkle with nuts.
8. With sharp knife, cut into bars while still warm. Let cool completely in pan.
MAKES 2 DOZEN

Cookier Cookies for Goodier Giving

Fill the prettiest containers you can discover with the prettiest Holiday cookies you can make (see Tips for Holiday Baking, page 4). These pretty-special presents are for pretty-special people: world travelers (actual or would-be); sophisticated niece or nephew; a beloved teacher; your husband's new boss; or anyone with a taste for the different and dramatic.

This enormous brown-and-white pitcher filled with Moravian Spice Cookies is fine for anyone with a feeling for the Provincial. And the Cinnamon Stars in the basket are fine for anyone's family or friends. So good! (You'll find the recipes on page 55.)

A word to the wise baker: You would be well advised to make extra amounts of all these fine cookies, for we give you fair warning that once your family gets a whiff of them baking, there'll be no living with them unless they have plenty of each delicious variety to nibble on all through the Holidays.

CINNAMON STARS

¹/₃ cup egg white (2 egg whites)	Granulated sugar
1¹/₄ cups granulated sugar	1¹/₂ tablespoons ground cinnamon
1¹/₂ cups unblanched almonds, ground	1 cup sifted confectioners' sugar
All-purpose flour	2 tablespoons water

1. In small bowl of electric mixer, let egg whites warm to room temperature – about 1 hour.
2. With electric mixer at medium speed, beat egg whites until soft peaks form when beater is raised.
3. Add 1¹/₄ cups granulated sugar to egg whites, 2 tablespoons at a time, beating after each addition. Continue to beat until mixture is very thick and glossy – about 10 minutes.
4. In medium bowl, combine almonds with cinnamon. Stir in egg-white mixture; mix to combine well.
5. Refrigerate dough, covered, overnight.
6. Lightly sprinkle wooden board or pastry cloth with flour and granulated sugar. Roll out dough, one half at a time, ¹/₄ inch thick.
7. Using 3-inch cookie cutter, cut out cookies. Place, 1 inch apart, on lightly greased cookie sheets.
8. Let cookies stand, uncovered, at room temperature, 2 hours.
9. Meanwhile, preheat oven to 300F. In small bowl, combine confectioners' sugar with 2 tablespoons water, mix until glaze is smooth.
10. Bake cookies 20 minutes. Brush tops with glaze; bake 5 minutes longer. Remove to wire rack; cool.
MAKES ABOUT 2¹/₂ DOZEN

MORAVIAN SPICE COOKIES

Cookie Dough

4 cups sifted all-purpose flour	¹/₂ teaspoon ground cloves
³/₄ teaspoon baking soda	¹/₂ cup light-brown sugar, firmly packed
¹/₂ teaspoon salt	¹/₂ cup butter or regular margarine, softened
1 teaspoon ground ginger	1 cup light molasses
1 teaspoon ground nutmeg	
1 teaspoon ground cinnamon	**Frosting**
¹/₂ teaspoon ground allspice	¹/₃ cup egg white
	3³/₄ to 4 cups sifted confectioners' sugar

1. Make Cookie Dough: Sift flour with baking soda, salt, and spices; set aside.
2. In large bowl, with portable electric mixer at medium speed, beat brown sugar, butter, and molasses until well combined.
3. With wooden spoon, stir in flour mixture; then mix with hands until well combined. Form dough into a ball. Wrap in waxed paper or plastic wrap; refrigerate overnight.
4. Next day, preheat oven to 375F. Lightly grease cookie sheets.
5. Divide dough into 4 parts. Refrigerate until ready to roll out.
6. On lightly floured surface, roll out dough, one part at a time, ¹/₈ inch thick.
7. Using 5-inch gingerbread-man cutter, cut out 12 cookies. Use assorted smaller cutters to cut out rest of cookies.
8. Place cookies, 1 inch apart, on prepared cookie sheets. Bake 6 to 8 minutes, or until lightly browned. Remove to wire rack; cool.
9. Meanwhile, make Frosting: In medium bowl, with portable electric mixer at medium speed, beat egg whites with 3³/₄ cups sugar, to make a smooth, stiff frosting. If frosting seems too thin, beat in a little more sugar. Cover with damp cloth until ready to use.
10. To decorate cookies: Pipe frosting through number 4 small tip for writing, following outline of cookies. Decorate centers of cookies as desired.
MAKES 1 DOZEN GINGERBREAD MEN AND 7 TO 8 DOZEN SMALLER COOKIES

GUMDROP BARS

1½ cups sifted all-purpose flour
1 teaspoon baking powder
½ teaspoon salt
1 teaspoon ground cinnamon
⅓ cup soft shortening
1 cup light-brown sugar, firmly packed
1 egg
2 teaspoons vanilla extract
¼ cup evaporated milk, undiluted
1 cup small, soft gumdrops,* cut into small pieces
½ cup coarsely chopped walnuts
Confectioners' sugar

1. Preheat oven to 350F. Lightly grease a 9-by-9-by-1¾-inch pan.
2. Sift flour with baking powder, salt, and cinnamon; set aside.
3. In large bowl, with wooden spoon, or portable electric mixer at medium speed, beat shortening, brown sugar, egg, and vanilla until fluffy.
4. Beat in half the flour mixture along with evaporated milk until smooth. Stir in remaining flour mixture until well combined.
5. Add gumdrops and walnuts, mixing well.
6. Spread evenly in prepared pan. Bake 25 to 30 minutes, or until cake tester inserted in center comes out clean.
7. Remove to wire rack; cool partially. Cut into bars while still warm. Sprinkle with confectioners' sugar.
MAKES 20
*Use any flavor except licorice.

FINNISH LOGS

¾ cup butter or regular margarine, softened
⅓ cup sugar
1 teaspoon almond extract
2 cups sifted all-purpose flour
1 egg, slightly beaten

Topping
¼ cup finely chopped unblanched almonds
1½ teaspoons sugar

1. Preheat oven to 350F. Lightly grease cookie sheets.
2. In large bowl, with wooden spoon, beat butter, sugar, and almond extract until light and fluffy.
3. Stir in flour; then mix with hands, to make a smooth dough.
4. Turn out onto lightly floured surface. With hands, shape into a roll 6 inches long. With sharp knife, cut crosswise into 6 parts.
5. Shape each part into a roll 12 inches long and ¾ inch in diameter. Cut each roll crosswise into 6 (2-inch) pieces, to resemble logs.
6. Place, 1 inch apart, on prepared cookie sheets. Brush tops lightly with egg.
7. Make Topping: Combine almonds and sugar; sprinkle over logs.

8. Bake 15 to 20 minutes, or until lightly browned. Remove to wire rack; cool.
MAKES 3 DOZEN

HOLIDAY FRUIT DROPS
(Pictured on page 59)

2 squares unsweetened chocolate
1½ cups sifted all-purpose flour
¼ teaspoon salt
¼ teaspoon baking soda
1 pkg (8 oz) pitted dates, coarsely chopped
½ lb cubed mixed candied fruit, chopped
1 cup coarsely chopped walnuts
2 tablespoons brandy (optional)
½ cup butter or regular margarine, softened
1 cup light-brown sugar, firmly packed
1 egg
1 teaspoon vanilla extract
½ cup buttermilk
Halved candied cherries or walnuts

1. Melt chocolate over hot, not boiling, water; let cool. Sift flour with salt and baking soda; set aside.
2. Lightly toss dates with candied fruit, chopped walnuts, and brandy; set aside.
3. In large bowl, with portable electric mixer at medium speed, or wooden spoon, beat butter, brown sugar, egg, and vanilla until smooth and fluffy. Add chocolate, beating until combined.
4. With wooden spoon, stir in buttermilk, then flour mixture, blending well. Stir in fruit-nut mixture.
5. Refrigerate dough, covered, 1 hour.
6. Meanwhile, preheat oven to 375F. Lightly grease cookie sheets.
7. Drop dough by rounded teaspoonfuls, 2 inches apart, onto prepared cookie sheets. Gently press a cherry or walnut half into center of each.
8. Bake cookies 10 to 12 minutes, or until lightly browned. Remove to wire rack; cool completely.
MAKES 6 DOZEN

CHRISTMAS BONBONS
(Pictured on page 63)

1. Prepare and refrigerate dough as directed for Holiday Fruit Drops, above. With lightly buttered fingers, shape dough into balls, using ½ teaspoon dough for each. Place, 1 inch apart, on greased cookie sheets.
2. Bake at 375F for 6 to 8 minutes. Remove to wire rack; let cool.
3. To make frosting: Combine 2 cups sifted confectioners' sugar with 3 tablespoons light cream and ¼ teaspoon almond or vanilla extract; mix until smooth. Frost tops of warm cookies. Dip in miniature nonpareils. Cool.
MAKES 12 DOZEN

The giant pine cone is really a jar that will serve many a purpose once the Gumdrop Bars and Finnish Logs, like those in the basket are devoured. ▶

HAZELNUT BALLS
(Pictured on page 42)

1 cup sifted all-purpose flour	2 tablespoons granulated sugar
½ cup butter or regular margarine, softened	⅛ teaspoon salt
1 cup finely chopped hazelnuts or pecans	1 teaspoon vanilla extract
	Confectioners' sugar

1. In a large bowl, combine all ingredients except confectioners' sugar. With hands, mix until thoroughly blended.
2. Refrigerate dough 30 minutes.
3. Meanwhile, preheat oven to 375F.
4. Form dough into 1¼-inch balls. Place, 1 inch apart, on ungreased cookie sheets; bake 15 to 20 minutes, or until set but not brown.
5. Let stand 1 minute. Remove to wire rack; cool partially.
6. Roll in confectioners' sugar while still warm; cool completely. Just before serving, reroll in sugar.
MAKES ABOUT 20

SPRINGERLE
(Pictured on page 63)

4 cups sifted all-purpose flour	2 cups granulated sugar
1 teaspoon baking powder	2 teaspoons grated lemon peel
½ teaspoon salt	2 tablespoons anise seed
4 eggs	Confectioners' sugar

1. Sift flour with baking powder and salt, twice; set aside.
2. In large bowl of electric mixer, at high speed, beat eggs until thick and lemon-colored – about 5 minutes.
3. At medium speed, gradually beat in granulated sugar, 2 tablespoons at a time, beating after each addition. Continue to beat until mixture is thick and smooth – about 10 minutes – occasionally cleaning side of bowl with rubber scraper.
4. Add flour mixture and lemon peel to egg mixture; with a wooden spoon, mix well, until it is smooth.
5. Refrigerate dough, covered, overnight. Also, refrigerate Springerle rolling pin.
6. Lightly grease 2 large cookie sheets; sprinkle each with 1 tablespoon anise seed.
7. Divide dough into 3 parts; refrigerate until ready to roll out.
8. Sprinkle pastry cloth or wooden board lightly with confectioners' sugar. Roll over dough, one part at a time, on pastry cloth, coating lightly with sugar.
9. With regular rolling pin, roll out dough, one part at a time, to a rectangle 8 inches long and 5½-inches wide.
10. Remove Springerle pin from refrigerator; coat surface lightly with confectioners' sugar. Starting from long side, slowly roll pin once, firmly and evenly, over surface of dough, to make designs. (If dough sticks to pin, peel off with spatula.)
11. With sharp, floured knife, carefully cut along lines in dough, to make individual cookies.
12. With wide spatula, transfer to prepared cookie sheets. Let stand, uncovered, at room temperature, overnight.
13. Next day, preheat oven to 325F. Bake cookies 15 minutes, or just until light-golden. Remove to wire rack; cool completely.
14. Store in tightly covered container 2 to 3 weeks before using.
MAKES ABOUT 4½ DOZEN

SPRITZ COOKIES

2 cups sifted all-purpose flour	1 teaspoon vanilla extract, or ½ teaspoon almond extract
¼ teaspoon salt	
¾ cup butter or regular margarine, softened	Cinnamon candies, angelica, miniature nonpareils
½ cup sugar	
1 egg yolk	

1. Refrigerate ungreased cookie sheets until ready to use.
2. Preheat oven to 375F. Sift flour with salt; set aside.
3. In large bowl, using portable electric mixer at medium speed, or wooden spoon, beat butter, sugar, egg yolk, and vanilla until smooth and fluffy.
4. Add flour mixture, stirring with wooden spoon until smooth and well combined. Fill cookie press with dough. Then make one or all of the following shapes.
5. Wreaths: Use star disk. Force dough onto cold cookie sheet in a 12-inch strip; cut strip into 3 parts. Form each part into a circle. Decorate with cinnamon candies and angelica.
6. Christmas Trees: Use Christmas-tree disk. For each, stand press upright on cold cookie sheet; force out dough, to form tree. Reverse handle of press slightly to cut off dough. Sprinkle the trees with nonpareils. The cookies should be 1½ inches apart.
7. Rosettes: Use a rosette disk. For each, stand press upright on cold cookie sheet; force out dough, to form a rosette. Reverse handle of press slightly to cut off dough. Cookies should be 1½ inches apart.
8. Bake cookies 8 to 10 minutes, or until light-golden. Remove to wire rack; cool.
MAKES ABOUT 4 DOZEN IN ALL

Happy the individual who gets the towering glass jar filled with Holiday Fruit Drops (recipe on page 56) and Spritz Cookies (above) and Brown-Sugar Shortbread cookies (recipe on page 62). The thoughtful giver might even attach a copy of the recipe.

CHOCOLATE RIBBONS

1 pkg (3 oz) soft cream cheese	**Glaze**
1 cup butter or regular margarine, softened	3 squares semisweet chocolate
1 cup sugar	2 tablespoons butter or regular margarine
1 egg yolk	Chocolate or multi-colored miniature nonpareils
1 teaspoon vanilla	
2 envelopes (1-oz size) no-melt unsweetened chocolate	
2½ cups sifted all-purpose flour	

1. Preheat oven to 350F. Refrigerate ungreased cookie sheets until ready to use.
2. In a large bowl, with wooden spoon or portable electric mixer at medium speed, beat cheese, butter, sugar, egg yolk, and vanilla until smooth and fluffy.
3. Add the chocolate; beat until well combined.
4. With wooden spoon, stir in flour, mixing until well blended.
5. Fill cookie press with dough. Force dough through ribbon disk, in 2-inch strips, onto cold cookie sheets. Use sharp paring knife to cut dough after each strip is formed. Strips should be 1½ inches apart.
6. Bake cookies 8 to 10 minutes, or just until set but not browned. Remove to wire rack; cool.
7. Meanwhile, make Glaze: Melt chocolate and butter over hot, not boiling, water. Mix well; cool.
8. Dip one end of each cookie in glaze; then dip in nonpareils. Return to wire rack, to let glaze set.
MAKES 12 DOZEN

CHOCOLATE COOKIES DE LUXE

1 recipe Chocolate-Ribbon-Cookie dough, above	½ teaspoon vanilla extract
2 cups sifted confectioners' sugar	1½ to 2 tablespoons milk

1. Preheat oven to 350F. Refrigerate ungreased cookie sheets until ready to use.
2. Prepare cookie dough as recipe directs.
3. Fill cookie press with dough; use a rosette disk. For each cookie, stand press upright on cold cookie sheet; force out dough to form a circle. Reverse handle of press slightly to cut off dough. Cookies should be 1½-inches apart.
4. Bake cookies 10 to 12 minutes, or until set but not browned. Remove to wire rack; cool.
5. Meanwhile, make Frosting: In small bowl, combine sugar, vanilla, and 1½ tablespoons milk, mixing well. (If frosting seems too thick, gradually add rest of milk.)
6. Fill center of each cookie with about ½ teaspoon frosting.
MAKES 7 DOZEN

CHINESE ALMOND CAKES

2½ cups sifted all-purpose flour	1 egg
¾ cup sugar	3 tablespoons water
¼ teaspoon salt	1 teaspoon almond extract
1 teaspoon baking powder	About 36 whole blanched almonds
¾ cup butter or regular margarine, softened	1 egg yolk

1. Sift flour with sugar, salt, and baking powder into large bowl.
2. Using pastry blender or 2 knives, cut in butter until mixture resembles coarse cornmeal.
3. Beat egg with 2 tablespoons water and the almond extract. Add to flour mixture, mixing with fork until dough leaves side of bowl.
4. On lightly floured surface, knead dough until smooth. Wrap in waxed paper; refrigerate 1 hour.
5. Meanwhile, preheat oven to 350F.
6. Form dough into balls 1 inch in diameter. Place, 3 inches apart, on ungreased cookie sheets.
7. With palm of hand, flatten each cookie to a circle ¼ inch thick; press almond into center of each.
8. Combine egg yolk with 1 tablespoon water. Brush on cookies.
9. Bake cookies 20 to 25 minutes, or until golden-brown. Remove to wire rack; cool.
MAKES ABOUT 3 DOZEN

The amber glass urn holds an ample supply of Chocolate Ribbons and Chocolate Cookies de Luxe; while the covered round basket's filled with Chinese Almond Cakes.

BROWN-SUGAR SHORTBREAD
(Pictured on page 59)

1 cup butter or regular
margarine, softened
1/2 cup light-brown sugar,
firmly packed

2 1/2 cups sifted all-
purpose flour

1. In large bowl, with portable electric mixer at medium speed, or wooden spoon, beat butter with sugar until light and fluffy.
2. With wooden spoon, stir in flour until smooth and well combined. Dough will be stiff.
3. Refrigerate dough, covered, several hours.
4. Preheat oven to 300F.
5. Divide dough into 2 parts; refrigerate until ready to roll out.
6. On lightly floured surface, roll out dough, one part at a time, 1/3-inch thick.
7. Using 1 1/2-or 2-inch fancy cookie cutters, cut out cookies. Place, 1 inch apart, on ungreased cookie sheets.
8. Bake cookies 25 minutes, or until light-golden. Remove to wire rack; cool.

MAKES ABOUT 5 DOZEN

SHORTBREAD STARS: Make dough as above, substituting granulated sugar for light-brown sugar. Use 1 1/2- or 2-inch star-shape cutters to cut out cookies. Bake as directed.

ITALIAN ANISE COOKIES

Cookie Dough
2 1/2 cups sifted all-
purpose flour
1/2 cup granulated sugar
3 teaspoons baking
powder
1/4 teaspoon salt
1 teaspoon ground anise
1/3 cup soft shortening

3 eggs

Glaze
1 1/2 cups sifted
confectioners' sugar
1 1/2 to 2 tablespoons milk
Few drops red, yellow, or
green food color

1. Make Cookie Dough: Sift flour, granulated sugar, baking powder, salt, and anise into medium bowl.
2. Cut in shortening with pastry blender, until mixture resembles coarse cornmeal.
3. Add eggs; mix with fork until dough holds together and becomes smooth. Then mix with hands until well combined.
4. Form dough into a ball. Wrap in waxed paper or foil. Refrigerate overnight.
5. Next day, preheat oven to 375F. Lightly grease cookie sheets.
6. Make Glaze: In small bowl, combine all ingredients to make a smooth mixture.

7. Divide dough into 2 parts; refrigerate until ready to roll out.
8. On lightly floured surface, roll out each part of dough, 1/4 inch thick.
9. With assorted 2 1/2-inch cookie cutters, cut out cookies. Reroll trimmings, and cut.
10. Using spatula, place cookies 2 inches apart, on prepared cookie sheets.
11. Bake 8 to 10 minutes, or until lightly browned. Remove to wire rack; cool slightly.
12. Brush tops of warm cookies with glaze. Cool completely.

MAKES 3 TO 3 1/2 DOZEN

CRISP NUT STARS

2 cups sifted all-purpose
flour
1 1/2 teaspoons baking
powder
1/4 teaspoon salt
1/2 cup butter or regular
margarine, softened
1 cup granulated sugar

1/4 cup light-brown sugar,
firmly packed
1 egg
1 teaspoon vanilla
extract
1 cup finely chopped
pecans or walnuts

1. Sift flour with baking powder and salt; set aside.
2. In large bowl, with portable electric mixer at medium speed, beat butter, sugars, egg, and vanilla until well combined.
3. With wooden spoon, stir in flour mixture and pecans; then mix with hands until well blended. Form dough into a ball. Wrap in waxed paper or plastic wrap; refrigerate several hours, or overnight.
4. Preheat oven to 375F. Lightly grease cookie sheets.
5. Divide dough into 2 parts. Refrigerate until ready to roll out.
6. On lightly floured surface, roll out dough, one part at a time, 1/8 inch thick.
7. With 2 1/2-inch star cookie cutter, cut out cookies. Reroll trimmings, and cut.
8. Place 2 inches apart, on cookie sheets.
9. Bake 7 to 8 minutes, or until lightly browned. Remove to wire rack; let cool.

MAKES 3 1/2 TO 4 DOZEN

A reproduction yellow Creil urn is crammed with crunchy-crisp Springerle (recipe on page 58) like those on the plate; while the small box contains Christmas Bonbons (the recipe is on page 56), plump and beguiling.

DANISH SPICE COOKIES

2½ cups sifted all-
   purpose flour
½ teaspoon ground
   cardamom
½ teaspoon ground
   cinnamon
½ teaspoon ground
   cloves
½ teaspoon ground
   allspice
¼ teaspoon salt
¼ teaspoon baking
   powder
¼ teaspoon baking soda
⅔ cup butter or regular
   margarine, softened
½ cup light-brown sugar,
   firmly packed
½ cup dark corn syrup
2 teaspoons grated
   orange peel
1 egg yolk
¼ cup ground walnuts,
   pecans, or hazelnuts
Walnut or pecan halves

1. Sift flour with spices, salt, baking powder, and baking soda; set aside.

2. In large bowl, with portable electric mixer at medium speed, beat butter, brown sugar, corn syrup, orange peel, and egg yolk until well combined.

3. With wooden spoon, stir in flour mixture and ground walnuts; then mix with hands until well combined.

4. Form dough into a ball. Wrap in waxed paper or plastic wrap; refrigerate overnight.

5. Next day, preheat oven to 375F.

6. Divide dough into 3 parts. Refrigerate until ready to roll out.

7. On lightly floured surface, roll out dough, one part at a time, ⅛ inch thick.

8. With assorted 2½-inch cookie cutters, cut out cookies. Reroll trimmings, and cut.

9. Place cookies, 1 inch apart, on ungreased cookie sheets. Press nut in center of each.

10. Bake 8 to 9 minutes, or until lightly browned. Remove to wire rack; cool.

MAKES 6 TO 6½ DOZEN